Confessions of a Tea Leaf Reader

by Tanya Lester

Confessions of a Tea Leaf Reader
Copyright © 2010 Tanya Lester

ISBN: 978-0-9692239-2-4

Are You Aware?
www.innercirclepublishing.com

This book is dedicated to Luke Alexander Lester, my wonderfully creative, insightful son, who patiently grew up to the murmurings of many of my tea leaf readings with clients in our living room. With love always, Mom

CONTENTS

Chapter 1

Giving In to the Temptation

A newspaper reporter who wrote a piece about me once began his article with the words: "The possibility of knowing the future can be tempting."[1]

And for me as the intuitive or psychic giving the reading—in my case, giving the tea leaf reading—to write about why people are tempted to come for readings, why they want to know so badly what is on the horizon, and what I tell them about it is extremely tempting for me. I am passionate about providing people with insights into their lives that will help them understand important aspects of their lives better and help them go forward into the future in a positive, even passionate, way. But I am also a rebel, and the idea of telling secrets is a very delicious idea for me to pursue.

Not delicious enough for me to want to hurt anyone, of course. This is why I have, in most cases, changed the names of my clients and not even bothered to mention the locations where the readings occurred. In some cases, I have changed details to protect identities.

---

[1] Timothy Schafer, "Exercise Intuitive Muscles at Tea Leaf Reading Workshop," *Nelson Daily News,* February 18, 2008.

I am very honoured to have input into peoples' lives in this way. What I see intuitively everyday is the magnificence of the human spirit. Among other things, I hope this book will encourage you to use your intuition more often, because if you do, you will truly see the rich character of each person with whom you come into contact each day, including yourself. You also will understand better how you can guide yourself through the twists and turns of your own life.

I never assume when someone walks through my door, in the upstairs apartment where I live at the edge of a village, that they know what tea leaf reading is. They often do not. Some have just a hazy idea of what it is. I will assume this is the same for you.

Seeing as every tea leaf or tea cup reader has an individual style, I will tell you that, according to the way I do things, I first ask the client to choose a cup. I have a variety of thirty or more. Each one has its own story of how it ended up on my side table. The wild little, green-and-yellow, handmade one was given to me by a young woman who could not afford to pay for a reading. It is ceramic, and she made it in a high school art class. Each time she visits me, she always checks in with it where I have it prominently displayed.

Another cup is a white one covered in a deep blue painting of an idyllic farm scene. I also got this one through barter. One woman who chose it said the image on the cup was a picture of the farm she envisioned having one day.

There is a tin cup with a cover on it, in white and aqua-blue, that I picked up in a secondhand shop. I guess it would be ideal to take on a picnic. Inside, the tin is a rich gold or brass colour.

Most dear to me is the replica of the blue cup I started out with. It has ocean images all over it. In fact, it looks like what you might see if you were swimming near the ocean bottom. There are angelfish, sea horses, shells, starfish, and seaweed on its sides and saucer. The background is a dreamy, misty-blue colour.

I ordered two cups like this from an Oxfam catalogue when I first got into tea leaf reading. It was from Thailand or Indonesia. I also got a sugar and cream set with the same pattern. Eventually, I was going to purchase the tea pot and everything else in the set, but Oxfam discontinued the line. Nowhere else could I find cups like these ones. They are extremely unique, I realized. I used the cups and saucers for a few years until they both broke, except one saucer. I was devastated and bought a solid blue cup to go with the remaining saucer so I could, at least, continue to use that.

I had an extremely strong connection to these cups. When I was making the agonizing decision as to which of two communities I should make my new home, I had a dream while visiting the community where I ended up living. In the dream, a loaf of bread appeared, which, to me, meant that I would always be able to feed myself if I moved to this community. Then, the blue cup that I had started tea leaf reading with appeared. This, to me, meant that I would have food (the earlier appearance of bread), and drink (the cup), and even the deeper level of spiritual "bread" and "drink." But it also meant, I believe, that I would make a living with my tea leaf reading. This is exactly what happened when I moved to this place. I made much more of my living from tea leaf reading than I did from writing, which had previously been my main income. My spirituality was also enhanced, not the least being from constantly practicing tea leaf reading.

So, when the cups broke, I was upset. But one of the cups was, in a sense, reincarnated back to me. It happened when I was invited to do a tea leaf reading workshop by a group of women in a neighbouring city. When I arrived, the host said she had brought some extra tea cups just in case I had not come with enough for everyone attending. There sat the replica of my blue ocean cup. When I told her my story, she said she had found it at a second hand shop and gifted it to me at the end of the afternoon. Miraculously, my cup was back.

****

So, someone coming for a reading gets to pick one of these tea cups, and every one of them has a story that goes with it. Some people ask if the chosen cup has something to do with the person who picks it or something about that person's future. Until recently, I have said no, it is just about having the enjoyment of selecting a cup. Lately, though, I have realized that of course the cup that someone picks has something to do with the person and the reading. There *absolutely* are no accidents.

Consciously, the woman who picked the cup with the traditional farm on it did it to encourage the Universe to manifest this for her. Subconsciously, I can understand someone picking my bright yellow cup with the blossoming flower on it because she or he will have a sunny future with full blooming sensuality and/or sexuality.

Once my guest picks a cup, I pick one for myself, too. Usually, I pick the first one my eyes are pulled to. I believe the Universe directs me in this way. I take the cups into my kitchen and fill them with the tea that I have already prepared.

Most of the time, I give my guest a choice of teas: black, green, or herbal and sometimes anything in between (e.g. oolong or white tea). The flavours of these tea categories are endless: cherry rose green, vanilla rooiboos, mint green, spearmint, and on and on.

Some tea leaf readers insist on using only one kind of tea to read. The best type is a point on which they disagree. Some say tea from East India is best. Others say Sri Lankan tea is superior, and so on. I find that I can intuit or read the clumps or leaves left in the tea cup after it is drunk regardless of what kind of tea is used. For example, a picture or image of a dog in a cup of black tea might look like a stick dog because the specks of tea are so small. With green tea, the dog will have "a lot of meat on its bones." But I can see both are dogs, and what it represents is probably the same regardless of whether it appears thin or fat.

By the way, I have seen dogs in cups for a number of reasons. Once, I saw a dog being watched by someone who wanted to kidnap it. Tact is important in communicating such findings in someone's cup. I work around to discussing something negative by saying something like, "Is the dog I am seeing yours? Do you have a dog?"

In this case, the woman replied that it was probably her daughter's purebred dog that I was seeing. She said she would go over to her daughter's house and let it out each afternoon. Immediately, a picture flashed into my intuitive third eye (the place in the middle of the forehead above the eyebrows). I saw her letting the dog out into the back lane and then going back into the house while it roamed around on its own, away from a watchful eye.

I said, "When you let the dog out, you might want to watch him because someone else, in a van, definitely is, and they might steal him."

****

Usually, I use loose leaf tea to do readings. In a pinch or an "emergency" (someone just *has* to get a reading and no loose leaf tea is available), I have used a bag of tea and broken it open into the cup. I remember once being at a weekend journaling workshop at a Benedictine nuns' retreat centre. To pass a Saturday evening, we broke open tea bags, and I did readings for other participants. The Benedictine nun who was leading the workshop smiled at what we were doing but quickly excused herself and scooted out of the room when asked if she wanted a reading.

Some religious groups are definitely opposed to tea leaf reading and other forms of divination. Some of these just condescendingly put it down as being a fun, trivial thing in which they do not really want to partake, and others get quite radical in their opposition to it. I remember that the tearoom where I did readings when I first started my career had a history of religious zealots picketing with signs outside the shop. The owner was an intelligent woman and called the police because she believed, and rightfully so, that they were harassing people going into the tearoom, and that is illegal.

Her compromise with religious groups was to not have a tea leaf reader on staff on Sundays. This was out of respect for a group of Catholic women who came to her shop after Mass on Sundays.

Once, when I was doing a tea leaf reading workshop, a Baptist woman attended. She expressed her ambivalence about being there by saying that she suspected I was running a "devil's workshop." She did stay and, ironically, was the most intuitive of everyone who was there. At the end of the workshop, she very sincerely told me, with a warm smile on her face, "I like you. I'm going to pray for you."

I liked her, too, and also very sincerely responded with, "Great. I can use all the help I can get."

****

You can as well use bagged tea in a different way for readings. Put the tea bag in the cup. Pour in hot water. When the tea has steeped, remove the bag and put it on the saucer. Drink the tea and when there is just a bit of liquid left, pick up the sodden bag on the saucer, break it open and dump the leaves into the cup. Drink the rest of the liquid and, presto, the tea leaves are in the cup and ready to read.

Sometimes, tea leaves from bags are very finely cut and, for this reason, are difficult to read. Or maybe the reader's eyesight is not good. Either way, you can use a magnifying glass to peer at the leaves.

****

Over the years, I have developed aspects of the tea leaf reading ritual that are, I believe, unique to myself and to those that have learned my techniques in workshop settings. (I think every tea leaf reader puts a personal "spin" on the procedure.)

After the client drains the tea cup, I ask that the non-dominant hand be used to turn the cup upside down onto the saucer—the non-dominant hand because that is connected to the intuitive part of the brain. This will help open the line of communication between the client and myself as reader.

Then, still with the non-dominant hand, the client turns the upside-down cup around three full turns on the saucer. This brings things into future time. It is almost like moving the hands of a clock ahead.

Three, of course, is a magical number on many levels—body, mind, and spirit; father, son, and holy spirit; and so on, back as far as the days when paganism was prevalent. Pagans believe the number three is important because the goddess Hecate is three-faced and represents the maiden, the matron (mother), and the crone (wise elder woman). She is a fertility goddess who is also the protector of witches. This is nice for me to know as many believe tea leaf reading and any divination is the profession of witches and I have no problem with being aligned with witches.

If the client wants a reading about his or her past lives or childhood, then I would ask him or her to turn the cup around three times counterclockwise. In this way, we would signal to the Universe that we want to go into the past.

Most people want to find out about their future. I usually start with reading about the present and going into the future. Some readers, who might be Buddhist or merely believe in the power of the now moment, do not really believe in the future. Divination for them means more about a deepening of understanding of what is going on right now or from moment to moment. Maybe, as well, it is more about the person's character, personality, emotions, spirituality, etc. This definitely comes out often in my so-called future-based readings as well. It is addressing, in a way, how the person can strive to be the best he or she can be and live their lives to their full potential.

Occasionally, someone wants a reading about the past. This does not happen often, but when it does, they are often quite powerful. (I mean here that the Universe very powerfully channels through me. I am not egotistical about the process. If anything, I have become more and more humble over the years after witnessing the incredible spirit of the many people who have come to me and the amazing power of our intricate and incredible Universe.)

I remember a young woman asking for a past life reading. The reading was like an overview of several of her past lives. In each past life, I saw through the images or pictures in the leaves a scene that showed me she led a variety of monastic lifestyles, which, of course, included celibacy.

"No wonder I like sex so much in this life," she said. It was a good insight on her part, because what someone does not experience in one life often will be part of that person's next life.

I remember another time doing a reading for a friend on her early life or childhood. She was in the second half of her life and said she could not remember what it had been like for her and wanted to fill in the blanks, in a sense. I saw things like how she interacted with her siblings and that she had spent a lot of time on the water. These things rang true to her based on where she knew she had grown up, her present relationship with her siblings, and so on.

****

Once the client has turned the cup, I ask him or her to put the non-dominant hand on the cup and to concentrate or meditate on something for which they want spiritual guidance. Sometimes, this would be the topic that motivated the client to come and see me in the first place. With children, I might ask them merely to make a wish. I assure the client that I will discuss a wide range of things coming up in the future but ask him or her to focus just on one aspect while the hand is on the cup. If someone cannot think of anything, I suggest that the client merely concentrate on having a good reading.

While this is taking place, I close my eyes and meditate for a minute. What happens next is sort of the signature part of my reading. No other professional tea leaf reader does this that I am aware of.

I do a sort of Reiki (energy healing) meditation and ask the Universe to assist me in providing an accurate and excellent reading for the client. Then, my spirit guides give me a picture that is connected to the client and often is a visual response to what the client is concentrating on. The picture I get is the answer. But, unless I really focus on it, I do not know the question or the topic on which the client has been concentrating.

One time, for example, I saw a client progressing up a ladder but moving from one side of one rung to the other side of the next ladder rung. I said to her that she was progressing in what she wants in life, but that it would happen in a roundabout way, not in a direct way of starting at point A, then going to point B, and then to point C.

Sometimes, the image that flashes into my mind is like a theme for the entire reading. I keep referring back to it as the reading unfolds.

If the person who wants a reading phones or knocks on my door or runs into me on the street and arranges an appointment ahead of time, I am able to sit down and meditate before the client arrives. (I prefer a Reiki meditation and, sometimes, will get into transcendental mantra meditation or a Buddhist follow-the-breath meditation also, but any form of meditation will work.) I meditate on giving the person an accurate reading, and often a picture is given to me at this point, too. It often will be moving, like in a slow-motion movie.

For instance, I once saw a star moving forward above the head of a client. I intuited that this meant that things would unfold for her in her best interest without her having to force change in her life. The star was a spiritual guiding light that she could feel comfortable following in a relaxed way. No need to get stressed out or to guilt trip herself about having to *do* something in order to move forward with her life. She could let go and let God or Goddess guide her.

I told her about this image during the reading. It kept being a reference point, especially at the end when she started to ask questions like, "Should I take a course? I feel like I should *do* something." I saw an image of her gaining wisdom in a circle of some kind. Perhaps even a book club. Also, there was an owl in the cup, which means a person is at the wise stage of life. I reminded her as well of the star and what it meant. No need to get formal about what she was to learn in this part of her life.

The rest of the meditation that I do before the client arrives helps relax me and clear my mind. Things like whether my son, Luke, is eating nutritionally, or has enough money, or whatever are put to one side of my mind so I can clearly focus on the reading.

****

I start the actual reading of the tea cup by looking at the leaf or clump of leaves closest to the rim of the cup. This is the image that will address what is happening in my client's life " right now," or what has just happened, or what will happen shortly. What I intuit at this point often anchors the reading, and from then on, the client relaxes into the reading. If I am accurate at this point, then I know I have the client's ear. She or he usually accepts me as a credible source of intuitive information.

When I first started doing readings, I remember, I went to the house of a client who was very intuitive herself and did readings of some sort. She told me I was accurate 67 percent of the time. Nowadays, when I channel the question to the Universe, I get the answer with a 92 percent accuracy rate. I know, over the years, my intuition has gone through many stages and opened up tremendously. I believe this is because the more I practice, the better I get at it. But also, other spiritual practices of mine, like Reiki, have brought out my intuition. They have given me more faith and confidence in what I am doing. Doubts can really make a reader flounder, I think.

From the leaf close to the rim of the cup, I work my way down to the bottom of the cup. This is an easy process if the leaves are mainly on one side of the cup all the way down to the bottom. As I progress, I get further and further into the future. By the end of the reading, I am basically one year into the client's future. This is a general rule that is often broken. I have had young women ask me how many children they will have. I might see someone having her first of two children five years from the time of the reading. Obviously, this has stepped way over the line of the one-year rule of thumb.

Sometimes, people have told me that what I predict for them happens, but it takes a year longer than when I say it will happen. Now, this has a lot to do with the fact that I go into a very spiritual place when I am doing readings. In the spirit world, there is no linear time.

Another intuitive suggested to me that maybe it depends on how enlightened the person is as to whether events happen at the time that I predict. There might be some truth to that, but it also could be a lack of humility on the part of the reader to think that it is somehow the client's problem if things do not happen on time.

I know many people tell me that things really do happen at the time I say they will happen. I sometimes figure out the time something will happen because there will be, for instance, a Christmas tree next to something I see in the cup. From this, I deduce it will happen in December or around Christmas time.

Often symbols that represent certain times of year, such as Halloween, Easter, and Christmas, also will appear in someone's cup, close to the top of the cup (the near future), when that time of year is coming up. For example, someone who gives generously to others might look like Santa Claus in the cup.

This leads me to another point I want to make. Usually, in tea leaf reading, a picture can be interpreted as literal as well as symbolic. It is an interesting combination of both. So someone who literally gives a lot to others can be seen symbolically as a Santa Claus.

****

After the reader interprets all of the leaves on the side of the cup, the next place to look is at the bottom of the cup. The leaves there are often about ongoing projects throughout the year. If someone will be involved in planning a huge family reunion, for example, the leaves might warn of differences of opinions with others involved in the planning, what kind of food will be served, where it will be decided in the end to hold the family reunion, who unexpectedly might come, etc.

To get back to time frame, sometimes when I am grappling with when something is going to happen, like when a woman will meet her true love, the printed word November appears on the "screen" of my Third Eye. It is much like the electronic digital device that tells the time and the day that you see on buildings in a city. Then, I say to the client, "November. You will meet him in November."

There is another very interesting way that the leaves can be read in order to get time accuracy on upcoming events. If the leaves are spread all around the cup, the reader can do what is known as a clock reading. S/he holds the cup by the handle, with the handle pointing towards herself or himself. The handle is the present time. To the left, one quarter of the way around the cup is three months in the future. Directly across from the handle is six months in the future. Halfway back to the handle on the right side is nine months in the future. Right next to the handle on the right side is a year in the future. So, seeing that someone will have enough money to go on a huge shopping spree by looking at a picture of someone shopping halfway between the handle (the present) and halfway along the left side of the cup (the three month mark) will mean that it will happen approximately a month and a half in the future.

Figuring out a pattern for the pictures in the leaves in the cup is a way to help the reader, especially a new one, to know where to begin and where to go next. Otherwise, staring at all those leaves in the cup can be totally overwhelming. Of course, the leaves do not necessarily fall in a neat pattern. Sometimes, they are all over the place, it seems. Then, I trust my intuition and go with whichever clump of leaves my eyes are drawn to and then wherever my eyes go next.

What I see is the client's mind, body, and spirit and those connected to him or her as they all head into the future. It is a mystical experience, and the stories are very worth telling. This is what you will be reading in the next chapters of this book.

Chapter Two

In the Beginning

The story that I have told most often because so many people are curious about it is about how I became a tea leaf reader. They often ask this when we are sitting together drinking the tea before the reading begins.

I have told this story thousands of times and almost as many times as I have given people readings. I know I have to tell it here, too, because people want to know.

Several times in my life, I have been called by Spirit to do something extremely important on a professional level. Tea leaf reading has been one of these callings for me.

Things began to fall into place for me to become a tea leaf reader years before I actually picked up a cup and did a reading. After I got my university degree in 1979, I spent a year away from my hometown. It was there that I walked into a hole-in-the-wall metaphysical shop one day.

Those were the pioneer days for metaphysical shops. Today, they sell clothes, shoes, jewelry, crystals, books, and every kind of divination tool under the sun. The shop I walked into, in 1980, had a few books spread out on a table and little else. The walls were bare.

But it was there that I found *Tea-Cup Reading and the Art of Fortune-Telling by Tea-Leaves by a Highland Seer with*

Ten Illustrations. Apparently, whoever wrote the book feared recrimination and so refrained from disclosing his or her name as the author.

The book had obviously been put together on a low budget—maybe because no publishing house wanted to take the risk of publishing something that was deemed to be on such a controversial or satanic topic. It had an orange cardboard cover (not as hard as and cheaper than the kind used for most mass produced paperbacks) and had ring binding to hold the pages in place.

I bought the book. Not for its attractive cover but because of its contents. Lots of people were reading Tarot cards already at that time. I always liked to be different. "If I get into doing readings, tea leaf readings would be more unique than Tarot," I said to myself. (It would be years before I realized that my family ancestry was really what was motivating me.)

I took the book home and never looked inside it for several years. Life intervened. In those days, my primary passion was writing. Travel was already starting to be a major interest, too.

Nothing was happening in the area of psychic development. Yet, there was still enough connection between me and that book for me to include it among the books and furniture and things that I brought back with me when I returned to my hometown. There, it ended up on a shelf for a long time. The only time I dusted it off and looked at its cover was when I would have a yard sale. "Should I just put this on a table with the other books I want to get rid of?" I would ask myself.

Something inside me would stir slightly. My arm would move and my hand would put the tea leaf reading book back on my shelf. Somehow, I felt, its time would come.

Seemingly unrelated, around this time, I got my Reiki I (energy healing) attunement. At the weekend workshop, I was paired up with a woman so we could practice this hands-on healing technique on each other. We became friends and met often to do Reiki exchange with each other. Reiki had (and still has) a profound effect on me. It built my confidence. The writing courses that I was teaching expanded, and I started to use its energy to relate well with the adults who took my courses. Things just went better.

Life always has its challenges, and I have had my share— sometimes, I think, more than my share—but I can deal with everything from this peaceful, calm centre. This is the Reiki energy, a spiritual force that buoys me through life. Anything I am passionate about, I can do. This is the Reiki influence.

So there are no accidents. There definitely was a reason for the woman with whom I did Reiki exchange to ask me to help her plan a tea party. Mary, I will call her, enjoyed making those amazing cakes filled with chocolate mousse and lemon fillings and strawberries. To have a tea party was a way that she could have fun with something she really enjoyed doing.

"Wouldn't it be great if we could find a tea leaf reader to come to the party?" Mary asked me one day.

We started searching for someone. We had one friend who was a Tarot reader.

"There is no way that I can read tea leaves," she said.

Something slowly opened up in my Third Eye. There was that book on tea leaf reading sitting up there on my book shelf. "You know, Mary," I said. "Maybe this is the time that I am supposed to start tea leaf reading."

I believe it was the Reiki that gave me the confidence. It gave me the confidence, as I will explain later, to make fertile a seed of natural ability that had been planted in me upon conception.

Each night, I read a bit of the book on tea leaf reading. When the day of Mary's party rolled around, I went to it with this book in hand.

I took a long time to do the readings because, each time I looked at an image in someone's cup I was reading, I had to stop and flip through the back of the book. Here, as in most books on tea leaf reading, there is a list of what different pictures in the leaves mean or how they should be interpreted. For example, an angel is listed as meaning "good news, especially good fortune in love." Seeing an axe, according to this book, means "difficulties overcome." If there is a boat in the cup, it means, apparently, that "a friend will visit," and so on.

Everyone at the party gave me encouragement. I remember giving a mother, who had a young son who was diagnosed with attention deficit disorder (ADD), information that she indicated was good advice. It rang true for her.

I just loved what had opened up for me. I was so into it, so passionate about it. It was like I was right inside that cup, like it was a whole new world that I had stepped inside.

Within a matter of a couple of months, I was reading professionally for money at a British-style tea room, complete with silver service.

Some of my friends, as friends will be, and family, as family will be, thought I had gone off the deep end. I was a popular writing teacher who worked with seniors who were writing their life stories and with others who enrolled in my creative writing classes at a university continuing education program. What was I doing by suddenly starting to read tea cups?

Over the years, I have come to realize the connection between being a writer and doing tea leaf readings. Both are about communicating, and I am a good communicator. Having gone through past-life regression sessions, I realize that, in one way or another, I have always been a communicator.

In one past life regression session facilitated by a guy I dated, I discovered that I was a princess in a past life. I lived in a desert setting, probably in the Middle East (I am of Lebanese ancestry on one side of my family in this life) in a castle.

I had the intuitive power to see if a man was committing incest. I would see a black sort of cloud around anyone who was a perpetrator. My father, the king, was a good, loving man. He allowed me to address everyone in the kingdom at the huge monthly assemblies. From the castle stage, he would speak to them about things of importance to the kingdom. During his speech, he would turn things over to me at a particular point.

I was a witness and pointed out every man in the assembly who was a sexual abuser. The whole idea was to single them out as a way to encourage them to feel remorse for hurting their children in this way.

Among other things, I was being a communicator in that lifetime just like I am a communicator in this lifetime—through my writing; my public speaking (as a writing and, subsequently, a tea leaf reading workshop teacher); and my reading (interesting word) of tea leaves.

Getting back to my friends and family, it did not really matter to me that they were not welcoming my change in life direction with open arms. I know that, to get the most out of life, each one of us often has to take huge risks and stand alone while taking those risks.

I was doing tea leaf reading workshops soon after I began to give readings at the British tea room. I was so filled with passion and confidence, and because I had been facilitating writing courses for so long, it was quite easy to start facilitating workshops based on this new life work of mine. Once you get the knack for teaching, then I think, in a way, you can teach almost anything.

Also, any teacher will tell you that the easiest way to learn about something is to teach it. And the easiest way to find out if something works is to try it out on your students if you are willing to take the risk.

Teaching the workshops was connected to helping me to understand that I had to work with my intuition if I was going to excel as a tea leaf reader (and later on as a channeller and Tarot reader as well). Right from the beginning, the workshops were a place for me to try things that helped me expand as an intuitive tea leaf reader.

Shortly after I started to do readings, something inside me—it was not really a voice, it was more a deep knowingness—told me that I should not use lists in books on tea leaf reading to help me interpret the leaves. Using my intuition instead of book definitions would tailor the reading to the individual. What I mean is, for example, in *Tea Cup Reading and the Art of Fortune Telling by Tea-Leaves*, seeing an aircraft in someone's cup is defined as meaning the person will be involved in "unsuccessful projects." But what if the person you are reading for is an airplane pilot? The aircraft is probably there to let you know, as the reader, this fact about the person you are giving the reading to. Other clumps of leaves nearby might provide information about something that is coming up in the pilot's work. In other words, the list definitions might be too narrow or totally inaccurate, depending on whom you are doing the reading for.

Also, I have seen a list in a book that included a "knight" among the definitions. In the thousands of readings that I have done, I have never seen the image of a knight. It makes sense. We do not live in an era of knights in shining armor.

But these kinds of entries in a definition list make me feel these lists were developed by individual tea leaf readers. Time and time again, a tea leaf reader would see a picture, and more often than not, it would mean the same thing over and over again. When the tea leaf reader made a list, the picture would be given a definition based on how often, when it showed up in a cup, it turned out to mean the same thing.

I can understand this from my own experience. Always, when I see a tree in someone's cup, it means family tree or related to family in some way. But it is my intuition that provides the details. I have seen a huge apple tree in someone's cup with images of friends in the branches of it. There were lots of apples, also, hanging off the branches. This client does not have a good relationship with her biological family members, so I intuited that her friends are her family. Also, she was looking for a home, and the tree represented finding a home (probably literally with an apple tree on it) in the fall because the apples falling off the tree showed it was time to harvest the apples, and that happens in the fall.

Other times, I have seen a tree and it has been about someone preparing her or his family tree or genealogy.

I have to add here, too, that I have seen a computer screen in someone's cup. None of the lists in books include the definition for seeing a computer. The lists were made before computers were developed. So, sometimes using your intuition means being able to give someone a complete reading by being able to interpret and discuss every picture seen in the cup.

For me to decide to go with my intuition was a very risky thing to do. As a child, and still as an adult, I always hated immersing myself into cold water. When I thought of just going with my intuition and not falling back on book definitions, this vision of diving off a pier into freezing cold lake water came to mind.

Still, I knew I had to listen to my intuition. I do these kinds of things. I believe I am courageous in this way.

But the spirit world likes to test us, I guess. Shortly after I made the decision to go with my intuition, I found myself reading a woman's cup in one of my tea leaf reading workshops. I even remember the room. It was set up for home economics classes in a high school.

The first thing I saw in the woman's cup, right near the rim of it, was the head of Mickey Mouse, the Disney character. I was embarrassed for seeing something so seemingly trivial in someone's cup. But I had to be true to my decision.

"Well, I see Mickey Mouse in your cup," I said, apologetically.

"Oh, yes," she said, smiling. "We just took our grandchildren to Disneyland."

There you go. "Go with your intuition" means have faith and go with it.

It makes sense, too, that I saw the Mickey Mouse image near the rim of the cup. This is where a reader usually starts the reading, and as I have said, it is about something that has just happened, is happening, or will happen shortly.

When my birthday came up on January 9 (I am a Capricorn), my friend Mary and I went to a restaurant to have a reading with a woman who had been giving readings for several decades. I had an agenda. I wanted to get advice from someone who had been doing readings for a long time.

The elderly woman came and sat in my booth and looked in my cup. "Well, you're a tea leaf reader, too," she said, with a look of surprise on her face as if she was thinking, "So why have you come to see me, then?"

"Well, she's good," I remember thinking before I said, "Yes, and I am just starting to do it, so I wonder if you can give me any advice."

She thought for a moment and then raised her pointer finger. "Well, one thing I know for sure—you don't learn to tea leaf read from a book."

"Thank you," I said. That was all I needed to know. She meant I needed to go with my intuition. What I already had intuited had been confirmed for me.

The thing that did surprise me about her, though, is when she said, "I never thought I would be doing this in my old age." I loved—and still love—doing the readings so much, it had not really dawned on me yet that tea leaf reading was considered trivial or unimportant or not-good-enough as a job or career path.

I have found out differently since then. A person either gets a big smile of delight on her or his face when I say I am a tea leaf reader or a smirk, which implies, "How silly," or "How crazy."

Once, a clerk in a clothing store responded with, "Yes, I fooled around with that when I was young."

"I chose to make a profession out of it," I shot back.

The woman who we went to for a reading on my birthday had a low opinion of herself for being a tea leaf reader. That surprised me, but since then, I have sometimes felt it, too. Friends and family members have sometimes preferred to introduce me as a writer or journalist instead of a tea leaf reader or a psychic. I think the term "intuitive" that is now often used by those of us in this field is an attempt to make what we do sound more credible.

Maybe for this reason or because I thought I might never be good enough at tea leaf reading, I kept going back and forth in my mind as to whether I should continue to tea leaf read or just drop it. Something my mother told me when I was about two years into doing readings made me definitely decide that I would continue with it.

My mother phoned me one day and told me that my grandmother and my great-grandmother on my father's side of the family were tea leaf readers. I was amazed. My grandmother, who we called Lala (her name was actually Lily or Laela Ateah Lester), died when I was five years old, so I cannot remember her ever doing a tea leaf reading.

My mother also told me that my great-grandmother Sophia Ateah always checked her tea cup first before doing anything of importance. This is similar to how people check in with a Ouija board. It made sense that she did. Living in the isolated community of Victoria Beach, Manitoba, which did not even have a road going into it, while she, with my great-grandfather Michael, was raising ten children, she had no one else, psychic or otherwise, to turn to when she needed to make a decision.

In any event, this information from my mother made me realize that I was destined to continue as a tea leaf reader. It was in my blood. The seed that had been ancestrally passed down to me had germinated. This is the Lebanese side of my family. (My great-grandparents came from Lebanon separately in the late 1800s. They met in Winnipeg. After a two-week courtship, they married.) One day, recently, I heard a documentary on CBC Radio about how Lebanese people, in general, are very interested in the occult and go often to psychic readers.

I think it was my practice of Reiki that encouraged this seed in me to start growing, and I think it has helped to strengthen my intuitive abilities. It also reinforces the affirmations or meditations I do in order to give people accurately intuitive readings.

Chapter Three

In the Very Beginning

According to the Internet, tea drinking began in China during the Tang Dynasty, which ran from 618 to 907 AD.

There is a legend that says tea drinking began with Prince Dharuma or Bodhidharma, the founder of Zen Buddhism, who went on a spiritual journey from India to China around 500 AD. He decided to sit for nine years and eventually went into a deep slumber. When he awoke, he was angry for going to sleep and cut off his eyelids. A tea bush sprang up where he threw them. So, from then on, the bush was a reminder of human weakness. It is said drinking tea strengthens resolve and diminishes the need to sleep. The tea ceremony is a beautiful part of Zen Buddhism.

The point I want to make in all of this is I believe tea leaf reading began where tea drinking started in India and China. The gypsies or Romas probably spread tea leaf reading and coffee grounds reading across Europe.

In the late 1980s, when I started tea leaf reading, a woman who came to one of my workshops talked about growing up in Britain. She was probably in her sixties at that time. When she was a child, she said, she remembered the gypsies coming and knocking on the door just when her family finished afternoon tea. They asked her mother if they could read the family's tea cups.

Something that an astrologer and Tarot card reader, who I will call Danelda, told me sheds light on the fact that tea leaf reading goes much farther back in my own Lebanese background than my grandmother and great-grandmother.

I was doing readings at a metaphysical shop when Danelda happened along one day. Almost immediately, upon being introduced to each other, she blurted out that she saw a gentleman who was one of my spirit guides standing next to me. I had no idea that he was there. She agreed with me that he was not one to draw attention to himself. "Now he is looking bashful because I mentioned him," she said. "He is a true gentleman."

I was more than intrigued. That night, before falling asleep, I closed my eyes, focused inside of my head, and asked him who he was.

He started speaking in a language I did not understand. (I later realized it was Arabic.)

"I don't understand the language you are speaking," I said.

"My name is Jacob," he replied, having switched to English. " I lived in the twelfth century."

"What did you do?" I asked.

"Oh, I lived in a hut at the edge of the village," he said, in a sort of rambling, storytelling way. "People would come to me, especially if they were lovelorn—had lost in love."

"Did you give them tea leaf readings?" I asked.

He hesitated. "Yes, but not in the formal way that you do," he said. "They would come and talk. I would stoke the fire and make some tea. After the tea was drunk, I would casually take a look in it and, guided by the leaves, tell them things. I was also an herbalist."

"Oh," I said. "What kinds of herbs?"

"Chamomile, peppermint, thyme, comfrey ..." he went on.

A few years later, I took a weekend workshop from Danelda, who is also an herbalist, in honour of Jacob. He has been a very quiet, unassuming, but tolerant and constant spirit guide over the years.

A long time after this, a client was complimenting me on my divination skills and mentioned that I was so unassuming. I like to think this is one of Jacob's influences on me.

This is probably a good place to tell the story about how Danelda possibly saved my life.

One day, I decided to take my son, Luke, who was in his early teens, up to Danelda's place for a reading. I was driving a station wagon beater ("an island car" they call this kind of vehicle where I live). The plan was to leave Luke there for a reading and come back later to pick him up and get a reading from Danelda myself.

I left the car to take Luke to the door, where Danelda was waiting. Wouldn't you know it? The old beater started to wheel itself down the hill. I dashed over to it, managed to get the driver's door open, and braked it. All three of us drew loud sighs of relief.

This thing about getting into accidents and near accidents had been driving me crazy. A car I had left idling had driven through the window of a secondhand store. When I was making a left turn one day, I did not see a car coming towards us in the left hand lane, and it smacked into the passenger side, where Luke was sitting. Once, when I was driving in the city, the bottom of the car's engine fell out. Neither of us had ever been hurt, but I did not understand why this kept happening. I was not a reckless driver. I did not think so, anyway. Of course, driving old cars that had not been repaired properly did not help. But still ...

When I finally sat down for my reading that night, Danelda had a great insight waiting for me. "In another lifetime, you were in a chariot accident and lost both of your legs," she said.

The penny dropped. No wonder I was so insecure about driving. After Danelda helped enlighten me, I did not get in an accident again, with two small exceptions.

Once, someone rammed into me while I was driving through a parking lot. It was unclear as to who was in the right and who was in the wrong, but the woman in the other vehicle interpreted it as meaning that she was supposed to get a reading from me.

I think she was right. She was in a bizarre relationship with a man who was probably enabling her to be an alcoholic. Later, she found out that he was having an affair with his daughter-in-law shortly after she gave birth to his son's child.

The other time was me backing into the bumper of someone's car parked behind me. This was shortly after the woman who lent me the car told me, in no uncertain terms, that I would have to pay the deductible if I got in an accident. I think this temporarily made me insecure about driving once again.

Danelda also had a great influence on my son, Luke. When he was around twelve years old, she told him during a reading that he was going to have triplets. Ever since then, whenever I have mentioned it, Luke responds, "Ha, that will get me into the Book of Guinness Records as the only man to ever give birth to triplets."

I always dryly respond with, "I think she meant your girlfriend or wife would be giving birth to them."

Whenever I run across Danelda, she always asks, "Has that handsome son of yours had the triplets yet?"

At time of writing, Luke is 22 years old, and we are still waiting.

But this chapter started out being about the history of tea leaf reading, so I will continue about that.

In my own research years ago, when I started teaching tea leaf reading workshops, I read somewhere that, in ancient Roman times, people would read the dregs in the wine—the grape stem and seed sediment left in the bottom of the glass after imbibing the wine. People tell me that there are still dregs in the wine, even today, when it is homemade. I look forward to having the opportunity to read wine dregs some day.

According to Joseph F. Conroy and Emilie J. Conroy, authors of *The World in Your Cup*, it is not known for sure whether the earliest civilizations practised tea leaf reading, but the evidence of bowls and bowl-shaped objects from those times strongly suggest that they did.

The father and daughter tea leaf readers write that the first records of tea leaf reading, or tasseomancy, appear in Sumeria, an ancient country located in the Middle East. They write that it was not tea but barley beer that was used for tasseomancy. It seems likely the bits of barley clinging to the inside of the drinking vessel produced images that were read.

Apparently, the Sumerians also looked for guidance into the future in cups of boiled bark and in the pieces of herbs from medicinal beverages. The latter divination focused on insights about the client's/seeker's health.

The Greeks saw prophetic symbols in the bay leaves in a bowl, while the Persians (Iranians) borrowed this practice and spread it through the Persian Empire and beyond.

In England, by the late eighteenth and early nineteenth centuries, people had realized that tea leaf reading was a good excuse for throwing elaborate parties. (I am regularly invited to do parties, and as the tea leaf reader, I am often the main source of entertainment at these gatherings.)

The Conroys go on to write that Scandinavians used different herbs for different fortune telling topics—one type for questions concerning love, another herb for health matters, and so on. I do not use different herbs or different kinds of tea based on the different themes that my clients want to explore. My readings are more all-purpose in nature. But many, many themes are covered in my readings. People have questions about everything under the sun when it comes to their present and future. I often say, "I have heard it all." But I know there is still something even more extraordinary that I will hear in the future.

Over the years, I also have met several tea leaf readers among First Nations communities, especially on Vancouver Island. Through my Third Eye, I see their ancestors reading the residue in the cup after having hot drinks made from herbs and berries that they gathered in the bush. Later, when trading with the Europeans began, they no doubt began drinking black tea.

It seems, regardless of our backgrounds, reading the leftovers from a drink of one kind or another occurs all over the world and has a long history.

Chapter Four

When the Future Concerns Death

Lots of people go for psychic readings, but I think among those who do not are people who have issues about death. These issues can include believing the intuitive might tell them that their death is imminent. This is also the reason why some people think fortune tellers are evil. They seem to believe that we are not seeing what is in someone's future but are actually creating it. Of course, we are *not* creating it. If we had that kind of power, we would be called God. Still, some people have this "kill the messenger" attitude towards us. (The assumption, as well, is that death is negative. My view on this has shifted since I began doing readings. My glimpses into the "afterlife" have made me realize that it is a wonderfully blissful place. Of course, we do not want people to die in pain, which is often what they experience before death. And, of course, we do not want people to die because we will miss them, but I believe that when someone dies, she or he goes to a better place.)

On the other hand, sometimes people come to us as a last resort because no one else can give them the answers they need to know. Sometimes, what they want to know is so difficult to deal with that I marvel afterwards at my ability to keep it together while I am doing the reading.

This was what happened when Rita came to see me.

She dropped in one Sunday afternoon at a metaphysical shop where I gave readings in the back room on a regular basis. A thin wisp of a woman, she told me that she was visiting from another town for the weekend. I started the reading by telling her something that I saw in the tea leaves concerning her daughter.

She shifted impatiently.

I was surprised. Most people are glad to hear about their children during a reading. As it turned out, Rita's personal concerns outweighed any concerns she might otherwise have had for her children.

I continued to read, hoping I would unearth something in the leaves that would resonate with her. "It seems you are having difficulties with your husband," I said.

"Now you're getting somewhere," she said, sitting bolt upright. "My husband tried to electrocute me."

I was stunned. My stomach tightened and I shifted in my chair.

She went on. "What I want to know is, did he consider killing me before that day when I was in the bathtub?"

Rita looked at me as if she were daring me to help her find the answer. I think she expected an excuse from me—expected me to mumble that I could not see anything or, even, that I was unable to go to a place so dark to help shed more light on what had been a completely devastating situation for her. I suspect other psychics she had gone to might have chosen to steer away from engaging in the kind of intuitive information that she obviously needed so badly.

I looked back into the cup for guidance. What happened is something that often happens when someone asks a specific question of me. A channel of information opened up for me.

I saw water. It is hard to explain how I saw it, but it was like it was around one of the clumps of tea leaves. "He considered drowning you," I said.

There was a flash of understanding and belief on Rita's face. "Yes, the day before, we went out together in our boat."

A voice in my head told me the rest of the story. It would have been very difficult to relate except that Rita was clearly indicating to me that she wanted to know the truth, the whole truth, and nothing but the truth. As with all my clients, I wanted to respect her by providing her with the truth even though what she wanted to know was not easy to deal with.

"He would have pushed you over the side of the boat, but there were too many other people in boats nearby," I said. "He thought someone might happen to see him do it through their binoculars."

Rita looked relieved to finally know. To know the truth, no matter what it is, is usually a great relief to people in strife-filled situations. (I know an astrologer who agrees with me on this.)

The rest of the reading was details. Her husband's adult children blamed Rita for his attempt on her life: a classic blame-the-victim scenario. I also saw they tried to cash in on the bizarre crime that had caused Rita so much pain. *National Enquirer*, the sensationalist tabloid, turned them down because none of them were celebrities.

On the positive side of things, I saw that her husband would get a longer prison sentence than her lawyer predicted. "Now that they have him in jail, they will find out he committed other crimes," I said.

Before Rita left, she told me that she had a new boyfriend who was a wonderful man. She also thanked me profusely. I remember her as a woman who had a lot of dignity. I respected her for this, especially after the ordeal that she had been through.

After a reading like this one, I have a bit of trouble with my policy of keeping readings confidential. I want to debrief with someone—get it out of my system instead of leaving it stuffed in the pit of my stomach. I wanted to share her story with the manager at the metaphysical shop, but I knew I could not. She had seen Rita coming in and leaving, so Rita's cover would have been blown.

After reflecting on the reading for a while, I realized Rita had wanted closure from the horrific experience she had been through. A therapist or her lawyer could not really help with this. And her husband was not about to cooperate with her wishes. It was only a psychic that could assist her.

****

Melissa came for a reading one rainy day in the late fall. Her partner had died suddenly of a heart attack several months earlier. I sensed that coming for the reading meant she was ready to go on with her life.

Things were progressing in the usual way: I read one clump of leaves and then went on to the next one until I came to the part about her becoming interested in having a relationship with a man once again before the year was out.

"I can't imagine that," Melissa said. "What would Joe think of that?"

Joe, I knew, was her recently deceased husband. She looked at me in a way that said she really wanted the answer. I knew that I had to shift to another place. I have had some training in mediumship (acting as the medium between someone who used to be in body and is now in spirit and someone in body who seeks information from someone in spirit), so I felt confident that I could give her the details she wanted.

I closed my eyes, and a voice I assume was Joe's (I had never met him) entered my head. "He says, 'It's my way of thinking that you need to go on with your life.'"

"What's it like where he is?" Melissa asked.

"It's my way of thinking that I can tell you how it is by saying this: I am with a group of five others. We are together and are asked to watch different people on earth. We are learning from this."

"What are they learning?" Melissa asked.

"It is my way of thinking (I was puzzled and even a bit embarrassed by the fact that I kept using this phrase because I never talk this way myself, but I was somehow compelled to keep using it) that it will lead us to a better place in the light."

"Has he forgiven me for the fight I had with him just before he left for work that day?"

The response, through my voice, was: "It is my way of thinking that, after all we've been through, why would I still be angry?" (Generally, I have found people in spirit do not harbour any anger or resentment that they may have had toward someone when the spirit was still in body.)

Melissa looked at me thoughtfully. "That is just the way Joe talked, and you know, it makes sense that he would be hanging out with the guys. That's what he did in life."

****

There have been other times, as well, when I have been sent a message from someone in spirit who wants to connect with someone for whom I am doing a reading.

One time, I remember seeing right near the rim of the cup (which tells me it is happening currently in the seeker's life) that the seeker's brother had something to say to her.

"Well, that's why I am in this city," the woman said. "I just attended my brother's funeral."

"There is something he wants to tell you that he didn't get a chance to tell you before he died," I said. "He will be trying to get in touch—probably in a dream."

Being a reader means sometimes having to think quickly "on your feet." If I did not have the confidence or if I had a problem with talking about death, I could have been very flustered by her revelation that the brother I was seeing in the cup had just died. I was able to quickly shift gears and deduce that he wanted to communicate from the spirit world.

In another reading, a woman in her early thirties, who I will call Rachel, asked me about two people who are now in the spirit world. I saw both of the peoples' spirits in a sunroom that must have been Rachel's. She did confirm that this is where most things happen in her home.

One was Rachel's mother and the other was her son. The mother suggested that, because Rachel had a new baby, she should make sure to take her family to the beach often and relax there.

Rachel confirmed that, when her mother had been alive, they often had gone to the beach together.

When she asked me to see if I could reach her son, I connected to Ricky, who I saw as almost a Dennis the Menace type little boy. His death had been a particularly horrible one for those witnessing and surviving it.

Rachel saw Ricky get run over by a stretch limousine and killed.

I could see Ricky's spirit also hanging out in Rachel's sunroom. He responded to her questions in the charming way that only a child can, using the slang that fits so well with being of a young age. It was delightful, really.

What turned out to be not so delightful was when Rachel sent her husband, Pete, to see me. "I want you to give me absolute proof, Ricky, an absolute sign that you are communicating with us," Pete demanded, his pointer finger grinding into the tabletop around which we sat drinking tea.

I could see Ricky, with his head down. He was tense with fear. I picked up the message that what his father was asking was too much for him. He did not know how to give "an absolute sign." His father was scaring him.

I explained to Pete that Ricky, in spirit, like Ricky who had been in body, was still eight years old.

Pete was relentless. He said the family thought the ice-cream containers' missing out of the refrigerator was Ricky's work.

I agreed that this seemed like something an eight year old would do. Pete, a grieving father, wanted more.

Finally, to move things along, I said Ricky would give him a more obvious sign in three or four days. I resolved to myself that I would send Reiki energy to make this happen if it was to everyone's greater good. It was a way to help me get out of the corner that Pete's aggressiveness had forced me into. This is the only time I have ever been concerned for my safety during a reading.

Then, I talked to a calmer Pete about the Spiritualist Church and how he could attend and work with mediums and healers there.

****

Bianca came to my home one day because she wanted me to help sort out why the spirit of a woman, whom she had never met but whose husband had performed in a dance concert that she had choreographed, persisted in "haunting" her. The woman had hanged herself.

We pieced together a solution to her problem rather quickly. Bianca had staged a production in which there was a segment when the dancers were hanging in the air with the use of a kind of wire prop.

I closed my eyes and channelled that the spirit actually thought she was in the afterlife. Based on how she had ended her life, it made sense to her that she would find herself with others who were also hanging (even if it was in a different sense than she had). To make it seem even more familiar to her, the spirit's husband was among those who were performing the piece. She was suffering from a "birds of a feather flock together" syndrome.

I suggested to Bianca that she tell the spirit that she had not yet reached heaven and to encourage her to go the light.

"Why didn't I figure that out myself?" Bianca asked me.

"You were too involved in the situation to intuit what was going on," I said.

****

43

Anna-Louise had a warm, generous personality but she was often depressed. Life is not easy for anyone who is disabled from birth.

My friend had never walked. As a child, she told me once, she was hauled around on a sort of cart or sled with wheels, pulled by one or another of her family members.

Clearly, she was born this way because her destiny was to improve things for the disabled and for those discriminated against for other reasons as well.

When Anna-Louise was awarded the Order of Canada for her work, she was met at the door of Rideau Hall by an apologetic Governor-General Ed Schreyer. His official residence, where the ceremony was to take place, was not wheelchair accessible. He outlined to her the plans he had to make it so.

Anna-Louise was a great portrait artist as well. She was also an avid animal lover.

The reading, one bitterly cold day, included an image or picture of a woman riding a winged horse or Pegasus. When I saw this, I thought it was heralding Anna-Louise's death.

This did not a surprise me in some ways because she had already lived more than a decade longer than the estimated 40-year life span medical professionals predict for those who have her condition.

Now, if there is anything that anyone wants to be tactful about in a reading, it is about death, especially when it just shows up in the cup without being specifically asked about by the seeker.

I took time looking carefully at this image before speaking about it to Anna-Louise. I thought it was her riding the winged horse, and I got the feeling she was being carried to heaven. But what if I were wrong?

Yet death, I have learned from personal experiences and from doing readings, should not be feared. And if Anna-Louise was to die soon, I felt she would experience total peace.

So, this is what I said to her: "You are coming up to a time now when you will experience total peace." I was playing with the truth, but I also was not prepared to tell her that I thought she would die.

Both of us had eventful lives and many, many friends, acquaintances, and, in my case, clients and students, so it turned out we did not talk again for several months.

When we did, she told me that she had been hospitalized because she had got pneumonia. With her condition, Anna-Louise had told me years before, getting pneumonia could easily mean her death.

So, the winged horse, with her on its back, had meant that she came close to death, but modern medicine had diverted it.

Wings in the tea cup, I find, often mean angels or spirits guiding us. Maybe an angel guided her away from death that time. And maybe it was some aspect of my intuition that held me back from telling her she would die when, obviously, it was not her time yet.

Years later, when I was living in another part of the country, I received a notice of Anna-Louise's death in the mail. I know the spirit of this good woman is at peace.

****

Soon after I started tea leaf reading, I did a tea leaf reading workshop at a seniors' centre. When I do workshops, at some point I always look at the leaves in everyone's cups.

In one woman's cup—who I will call Gillian—I saw a bed with someone stretched out on it. I *felt* that the person on the bed was very ill.

"I see there's someone in your life who is quite sick," I said.

"Yes," she said, meeting my eyes with hers. "Is he going to die?"

Like Rita, who I wrote about earlier, Gillian, I knew, definitely wanted the answer. A short sort of "psychic film" (that is often triggered by the leaves or by questions the client might ask when I do readings) started to play out in my mind's eye.

I saw a man desperate to die as an escape from the pain and discomfort he was feeling. I saw Gillian, who was worn ragged from caring for him and who knew the best thing for him would be death.

"Will he die soon?" I silently asked God and/or the Goddess, who I believe is ultimately the one who channels the information I require when I am doing readings. The answer I got was: "Yes."

"I think he will die soon," I told Gillian.

I should mention here that, quite often, when I do readings, I tap into the emotions that the client is feeling or will be feeling when something I am predicting will happen. I believe that we can be telepathic not only through seeing pictures or slow motion pictures but also through feeling. Picking up on the emotions I am getting when looking at a clump of leaves is part of how I can predict what is happening or is going to happen in someone's life.

****

Another time that I saw death in someone's cup was when I was doing readings as part of a bazaar at a community centre. I remember it was quite an informal atmosphere. We did not even have chairs to sit in as I read. Lots of people were coming and going. Not the ideal place for me to concentrate, and that is exactly what I needed to do when I saw what was revealing itself in the cup.

I glanced at the elderly woman standing across from me. Then, my eyes darted back to an image in the leaves that told me one of her grandchildren was going to die. What I saw was a cross and what I sensed was water. Her grandchild was going to drown.

I considered my options. If I was mistaken and the grandchild had already died, with the image showing up in the cup because the woman was still mourning the death, then there was no use in me bringing it up and adding to her pain.

But, if it was still to happen, then what a responsibility to put on her shoulders. She could go mad trying to prevent the death from occurring.

Yet, maybe through her free will, she could prevent it if I gave her the warning.

I ended up telling her that she should be extra watchful when caring for her grandchildren, especially if they were going swimming. I hope, if warning was needed, that this was sufficient.

****

At other times, I am pleased to say that I might have helped prevent death or serious injury. One time, I told a client, whom I will call Wilfred, that he needed to be careful when driving down the country road near his place.

As often happens when I do readings, a few weeks later, the follow-up phone call came.

"It happened." I recognized Wilfred's voice on the other end of the line.

"What?" I asked, trying to sort through my memory to connect with what he was referring to.

"I was driving from my place into town," Wilfred said. "I came up really close to a truck ahead of me. It was filled with steel pipes. A voice in my head told me to slow down, so I did."

I was holding my breath by now because I had by this time recalled that I had predicted a car accident during his last reading.

"Then, suddenly, one of these pipes rolled off the back of this guy's truck," Wilfred said, pausing for a moment for effect. "You know, I am sure it would have smashed through my windshield and gone right through my chest if I had not slowed down and stopped tailgating."

****

Felicity phoned me one day because she wanted to see if I could give her any information concerning her cat. Her two cats had wandered out of her yard one day and had not returned. After putting up posters, she had been contacted and had identified the body of one of her cats. It had been run over and killed on the highway.

"Should I keep looking for the other one?" Felicity asked me. "I am wondering if you can channel as to whether she is dead, too, or not."

I told her that, in the past, I had not had good luck in trying to intuitively locate lost animals. But I was willing to try again. I always like to help my clients if I can. As well, I always like to find out if I am able to do something that I have not been able to do before. I like to branch out, if I can. Sort of like a car mechanic seeing if he or she can fix a truck run by a diesel engine. Doing a lot of readings has definitely helped me expand my intuition over the years, so I am always willing to give it a new test.

I sat down and saw that the cat was getting fed by someone who lived five houses down the street from Felicity's place. I hoped I was not only imagining I was seeing this as, so often, neighbours do feed a cat living in the area.

For what it was worth, I called Felicity back and told her what I saw.

She got back to me a couple of weeks later. She had found the cat, not five houses down but fifteen houses down the street. I wondered if I had seen five and not the one which would have made it fifteen.

"You know, because you saw that she was still alive, that's what gave me hope and encouraged me to continue to look for her," Felicity said.

This was encouraging news for me as a practicing psychic.

More recently, someone named Millie asked me to call in the spirit of her cat. As soon as she asked this, I saw that her cat was still alive, and I blurted this news out to her.

"Yes," I said. "I see someone else took the cat in. She is a woman who lives alone and was very lonely until your cat came into her life."

"I put up posters everywhere," Millie said.

Then, I saw that the woman who had taken in the cat had seen the posters, but she was too enamoured with the cat to give her up.

Millie came back to me a day later and asked me if I could come up with the address and what the house looked like. I saw it was light blue and gave her the number. I was seeing the house as being in a different town than the one that Millie lives in. I think Millie did not see that as a possibility.

A few days later, she came back to me again. She told me the cat loved to be outside. Millie said she was always cleaning the cat because the animal got so muddy being outside. "That cat would not stay inside," she said.

I assume Millie was doubting that my divination was accurate (which some people do, of course), but I knew what I was seeing. It was only a week later, when I was home again, that I had time to reflect. Companion animals often take on the personalities of their owners. Millie is a wonderfully outgoing person with a tendency to be messy. I intuited that the cat was acting differently (had lost her desire to be outside) because she was now with a woman who is introverted and very tidy.

****

Through the experiences I have had giving readings to people connected to the different sides of death, I am more able to understand the adage: death is a part of life.

Chapter Five

Star Crossed Lovers

Questions about love relationships are part of the majority of readings that I do. Sometimes it takes an entire reading to discuss the intricacies of being in love. This is probably the most difficult thing to accurately predict. I guess it is because it is about two people, and usually only one is sitting in front of me and asking about it.

Also, sometimes my readings are about having options. The reader has a choice of which way to proceed. I might see that the best path for her to take is with the blonde guy, but she is bound and determined to go down the other road with the black, curly haired man. Desire, and especially our libido, can take us right off track.

Of course, sometimes we go and get guidance from the tea leaves (or Tarot, or pendulum, or astrology, or numerology, or whatever) when we have already started to wade into the relationship. We have gone in too deeply already to want to turn around and go back to safe ground.

I know this personally. Shortly after I started dating a very big man I will call Walter, I read his tea leaves. What I saw was one huge image. Seeing one huge image in the cup indicates to me that whatever the leaves want the client to know is of utmost importance. It is like a flashing neon light that says, "Take this very seriously."

The huge picture in Walter's cup was that of a big tree that looked like a big man being pulled out of the ground by his roots, as in tree roots. Whenever I see a tree in someone's cup, I always assume that this is about the family or the family tree.

Walter insisted that what I was seeing—that something happening in his family had totally "pulled him out by the roots"— was not true. My intuition told me otherwise, but I chose to believe him because I wanted to be in a relationship. It was for quite a shallow reason. I wanted to have someone with whom I could go out to social events.

Eight months later, I totally realized that I should have believed the leaves. He told me there was incest in his family—that he had had sex with two of his sisters. During our time together, I kept having flashbacks about my own childhood, including my feelings of disgust for the family that lived next door to me while I was growing up. In that family, almost everyone committed incest with everyone else. This is how intuition works, too. My intuition was sensing things that Walter was not being honest about.

This kind of thing is crazy making. People need to know that lying can really unbalance the people affected, especially if their intuition instills them with a sense of knowingness. The intuitive person flips back and forth and does not know which to believe: the intuition or what someone else is swearing to be true.

I believe your intuition is almost always right. This has been revealed to me time and time again.

Seeing as I am on the subject of lying, I may as well write about something I have noticed with a couple of clients. This does not happen often, but I have discovered that some of them lie to me, or at least fail to reveal to me the whole truth.

Some of them do this as a way to see how good I am or if, in fact, I am psychic. When someone asks me a question, I answer based on what the person asks. I do not have the time to ask Higher Power, every time someone gets a reading from me in which they ask a question, as to whether the person is being honest in what they are asking. Nor would I want to. I want to assume that people are honest. Otherwise, I would be suspicious of everyone who came for readings from me, and that would be a negative way for me to go through life.

Once, when I was giving a reading to a young woman, she asked me *if* she was going to have any children. I said she would have two children. Her mother, who was there, said, "Georgia, why don't you tell her that you already have a child?"

Georgia replied, "Other psychics have said I will have two children." In other words, she felt I had passed the test (although her mother did not seem convinced).

It was only later that I realized, by asking me *if* instead of *how many* children she would have, she was misleading me and being dishonest.

Getting back to Walter: it turned out he was very mentally unbalanced and on heavy medication and recreational drugs because he had not come to terms with what happened in his youth. He was not relationship material.

In short, I should have "listened" to what the leaves and, indirectly, my own intuition or channelling was telling me.

****

While I am on the subject of how my tea leaf reading has impacted my love life, I will tell you the story of Lars. We hooked up because of a prediction by another psychic, a channeller whom I met during a holiday on the West Coast.

During my session with Diana, I asked who was going to be my next lover.

"He will be dressed in green," she said, "and he will be so tall, you will have to use a ladder to kiss him."

I returned to a bitterly cold spring on the Prairies. The first day I was back, I was walking down the street right by my house when a man passed me. I was slightly acquainted with him and knew his name was Lars. I also knew he lived near me and wrote a column for a local metaphysical newspaper. We quickly said hello, and because it was so cold, we did not linger but kept walking—he down the street, me through my gate to my house.

Then, as if an angel wanted to show me something important, I spontaneously turned and looked at his disappearing back. He was dressed from head to toe in green, including an army parka, with the hood pulled over his head.

"He will be dressed in green and he will be so tall ..." I noticed for the first time that Lars *was* really tall.

A couple of days later, encouraged by Diana's prediction, I did something that I had never done before. I looked up Lars' phone number on the bottom of his column in a New Age publication and called him. I actually said that we should get together as I thought he was the man that the psychic had prophesized was supposed to come into my life.

Lars invited me over to his place to look at his book manuscript. When I got there, he told me about the renovations he was doing inside his house. I clearly remember standing next to him in the hallway and looking through the open door into the bathroom. A step ladder was sitting there as he had just finished painting the walls.

I looked up at him—way up at him. "... and he will be so tall that you will need a ladder to kiss him."

The Universe provided me with an interesting lesson about tea leaf reading through my connection with Lars.

Let me say that I was already planning to move to another part of Canada when I dated Lars and I had another love interest where I was heading, so I knew this was not a long-term romance between the two of us.

As for Lars, he was not in a good place in his life when I knew him. He was longing for a woman that had broken off with him after they were three weeks together but who he thought was the love of his life. He also had no money (she did), was not working, and was confused as to what he wanted to do with his life.

When we did the reading, he first wanted to concentrate on his love life. He concentrated on being with the woman he claimed to love. I read the leaves and saw that things would go well with this woman and him.

Lars then boiled the kettle again and made more tea in the cup I had read. He wanted to show me that he could manipulate the result—that not only his love life would go well but that he would get work that would make him a lot of money. The leaves would concur because that was his mindset. Then, presto, his whole life would be good in both of these important areas.

He drank the new cup of tea. He gave me the cup to read. For a moment, I saw the leaf patterns about his love life in the cup and the new leaves that would address the way to improve his financial situation through work.

We were both looking at these leaves. Suddenly, the leaves about his love life fell away. We looked at each other in astonishment.

He was no longer concentrating on the leaves in reference to his love life, so it was as if they were no longer willing to play the game.

My conclusion in Lars' case: the Universe was not willing to give him everything he wanted through manipulation. He could not just get the leaves to say his life would be perfect because that was his mindset and that was what he wanted. When someone goes to get a reading, she or he has to be open to what the Universe, with its omniscient power, wants for the seeker. If you manipulate the results based on your desires, you will receive a false reading.

This reminds me of another client I have who is always trying to manipulate readings, too. Joseph will phone in a positive frame of mind, and everything he asks comes out positively. Time and time again, I got that he would be making millions of dollars any day now. This has been going on for several years, and he has gone from bad to worse financially.

I just want to add here that, in many readings I have done since, the leaves have fallen away after being read. In most cases, no one has been trying to manipulate the results. It's as if the Universe wants to rest after its work is done.

To end my story about Lars, I have to say that we did not part on the best of terms. This was due to a problem that arose concerning a crystal ball that he lent me. It was a beautiful, big crystal ball— the classical type that is featured on the reading table of gypsies in pictures. When I gazed into it, trying to do a reading for myself with it, the images I saw looked ancient—that is the only way I can describe it.

It was difficult to intuitively read what these images I was seeing meant, but I was totally intrigued. I did some research on crystal ball reading and found out that, in order to bond with the ball, the reader was to merge with the ball's energy by sleeping with it. (I kid you not.)

I started doing this, so when Lars and I broke things off (I was moving away soon) and Lars wanted the crystal ball back, I put up a bit of a fight. After all, I was already sleeping with it.

Lars finally guilt tripped me into returning it, via his new lover, when he told me I would get into trouble on a karmic level if I kept it.

****

But getting back to the subject of love (and away from my personal love life for a while), I remember a telephone call from a woman one day who said she had had a tea leaf reading from me a decade earlier. "Of all of the readings that I've had, including the Tarot readings and everything else from different psychics, yours was the most accurate," Monique told me.

I had told her the man that she was going to marry would have certain initials. She told me that, in fact, the man who she was now married to and had two children with had the initials that I said he would.

But she had come back to me because there was a problem in their relationship. Monique did not really like having sex with her husband, even though he was a good-looking man. What came out in the reading was the fact that he was the type that was into having sex and then quickly getting on with his life. He told her that she was just making excuses when she said she did not like sex with little foreplay. That she needed to deal with the reality that she did not like sex.

Intuitively, I got that sex, at least in Monique's case, was a continuum that could start with touching and feeling good with her body and having it touched. This would lead to her enjoying sex.

I saw getting massage from a massage therapist could help her progress to good sexual relations.

After that, she sent lots of young women with relationship problems to me. One, I remember, was unhappy because both she and her boyfriend had "cheated" on each other, and she believed it should end between them because they no longer had any respect for each other

****

I gave quite a few readings to a woman named Jane. When she got pregnant, I knew that she actually was still in love with a previous partner, not the one who was the father of the baby. The man she was infatuated with was called Chad, and his problem was that he was a womanizer.

Part of Jane wanted to move back to the mountain community where she had previously lived with her daughter, and another part wanted to stay in the town where she then lived and where Chad lived.

She also had a strong desire to be an architect, and from the first time I gave her a reading, I saw that she could succeed. What always seemed to get in her way were the men in her life.

This happens a lot to women, and it is brought home to me so often in readings. To be in a relationship or to have a successful career still often seems to be an either/or situation for women.

With Jane, I had seen that if she went to the mountain community, there would be a man there—a tall man who would be more than willing (even financially) to help her to realize her dream. She should go back there, I urged.

I knew that she got pregnant on the same day that a very dear woman friend of hers had died. When she told me this, I counseled her to have the baby because the circumstances seemed too synchronistic to deny. When I looked in her cup, though, I saw that she should have an abortion and go on with her career. On the other hand, I did see that the man—we'll call him Ted—who had made her pregnant would not continue to have a relationship with her if she had the abortion.

A while later, I saw her with this man Ted. I had not realized this was the man she was with. I knew him a bit and I knew that he lived in a cabin on a mountainside. It dawned on me that this was the man that I saw would help her with everything she wanted in her life, but he lived in the town where we lived. He did not live in the mountain community where Jane wanted to return. Perhaps she thought it would be like living in the mountain community that she loved if she was with him.

Of course, something else could have been happening. Sometimes, a client will meet someone who fits the description in the reading but is actually a forerunner to the person who I see will be good in a relationship. Maybe the fact that I saw this man in the mountain community was an important factor.

Jane ended up having the baby and living with Ted for a while, and then they split up. Our lives are complicated. I often get things really accurate in readings, but it is very difficult to read all the twists and turns that happen in relationships. Also, some relationships have many more twists and turns than others. I always say relationships—especially if someone is destined to have a relationship with a specific person—are the most difficult things to predict. There is another person, someone who is *not* getting a reading from me, who is involved.

****

Not that it is always easy even if both people in the couple come for a reading together. I remember giving readings to each of a couple in a tea room once. Just from looking at the two, I picked up intuitively that they should not have been together. I remember thinking, how can I tell this woman (I was reading her cup first) that she should end it with the man sitting across from her when he was sullenly staring at me.

Another couple came for joint relationship readings from me several times. (I do this by asking both people in the couple to each put a hand on the turned-over cup at the same time and to both concentrate on finding out about their relationship while their hands are placed on the cup.) While they were courting, I saw they would have a wonderful life together travelling and living in different parts of the world. I saw that their children would be very special, very spiritual, I seem to recall.

They did get married and moved away, and he did a lot of travelling. She chose to stay home and care for their baby. Tension developed between both of them. They came back to Canada. When they came for a reading, I did not pick up on the problems in their relationship. When I had done the earlier readings, I saw they would have a good marriage, but what I was seeing spanned over a long time. Maybe it would have been different if she had travelled with him, as that is how I saw the two of them being happy. We can choose to alter what the psychic sees as what is supposed to happen or what is the best path to take in our future, but then we cannot necessarily expect the same positive outcome. It is intuitive guidance after all.

Or maybe their relationship problems were to last for such a short time that they did not even make themselves known to me when I saw a wonderful relationship over many, many years.

Or maybe I just became intuitively blinded to the fact that they had problems because I had come to see them as a happy couple over all the time I gave them readings. Sometimes, I find that it is best for people to ask me specific questions to which I channel the specific answers, especially if they are regular clients. This seems to break the spell if the reading in the tea leaves or Tarot seems to be not as accurate as usual. If someone is or becomes skeptical about the accuracy of my tea leaf readings, I sometimes find giving them a Tarot reading, from which they see the pictures on the cards, provides them with more "proof."

Then there are those who get readings from me because they have too many choices for love relationships. One woman was grappling with the problem of choosing one of three men. Now, I know many people might say, "Wish I had that kind of problem." But the woman who called me about this was really stressed out. She knew them all and did not want to hurt any of them. At the same time, she wanted the right person for her and her children. The confusion she was feeling by being unable to make a choice was really making life difficult for her.

This kind of reading for me is often quite easy. Either through tea leaf reading, Tarot reading, or channelling, I ask the Universe which one is the best choice for the seeker. In the tea cup, I will see each man and get information about him. For example, Joe is a hard worker. Bill is a passionate lover. Pete is good around the house and loves children. If I am using Tarot cards, I will pull a card for each one, and it will reveal their attributes. Then, I channel and ask the Universe, "Is Bill the best one to be this woman's partner? The Universe will respond with "yes" or "no." Or I see all of them in different parts of the tea cup, and I describe what I see about each to the seeker. There are variations on how I do this, but generally, this is the technique.

Of course, some people seem happy to continue to be confused about choosing a fulltime partner. One man, I remember, was getting free rent from one woman who wanted to be in a love relationship with him, but he was traveling with another woman. Before he left, he hinted that he might be open to adding me to his entourage in exchange for providing him with a place to stay in my town. (It was a place he liked to visit.)

He was attracted to me because, when I did his reading, I got the information that he would like to be involved in space travel. "Nobody knows that about me," he said, eyes and mouth wide open.

He found this very attractive. And men do find intuitive power in a woman to be very attractive, but scary, too. They are often drawn to it but will feel uncomfortable with a woman who "knows so much," maybe even more than the man knows (sexism still happens in our world). I know many seers who are single.

****

Boris is a good case in point when it comes to those being attracted to psychics. And if this is to be a book of true confessions, I have to admit that this was what attracted him to me over several years, on and off, while I raised my wonderful son and did not have time for or want a fulltime relationship.

Boris has always had an interest in the power that psychics have in being able to predict the future. He arrived in Canada from a communist country as a young man after defecting from a ship where he worked as a sailor. Before leaving his homeland, he was approached one day by a gypsy in a college café where he was studying. She said she would read his fortune in exchange for a few coins. He agreed. She proceeded to divine what would happen to him over a span of several decades and included the fact that he would live in a foreign country, marry twice, and have one daughter. When I first laid eyes on Boris, he was in his fifties, and according to him, everything the gypsy had told him came true.

I know that, when I read his cup, he was in awe of me. This is what attracted him to me besides the fact that I do have a unique look. No doubt, I was telling him things that really rang true. (Most of the time this happens when I give readings. I am a channel through which a higher power sends messages to my client; or you can call me a clairvoyant—that is another way of looking at it). And I think, for men like Boris, the process is very intimate.

And often, men, especially the type like Boris, only experience this kind of intimacy with a sexual partner. The spiritual aspect of it is attractive and seems very sexy.

Also, men tend to not express their inner feelings, conflicts, and dreams in the way that women do. To have a woman tell them something that they have never really told anyone before is something they find extremely attractive, I think.

I actually saw myself in his tea leaves. This has not happened often, but when it does, I usually do not tell the man in question that I have seen myself. I figure, if I did, they would just think I was trying to make a pass at them in a devious sort of way or (and this would be much worse) that they would question my credibility as a psychic.

It amused me when I saw myself in Boris' cup. He had been heading out to the United States to visit a friend and had coyly asked me, when I was giving him a reading, if he would meet any women there. I saw myself and so realized that this meant he was not going to pick up any women there. Maybe he liked me better than he let on. So much for his well developed Casanova reputation.

He kept me up-to-date on the accuracy of my readings as things I divined happened to him. Boris told me more than once that, if we ever lived together, he would find it very scary.

"Why?" I asked.

"You would know if I was ever interested in any other woman," he said.

He was probably right.

****

People often invite me to events because, even if they do not believe in the intuitive, they believe a psychic adds pizzazz to whatever the occasion is. I have done readings at a stagette (I am proud to say that the group of women who planned the event chose me instead of booking a male stripper for the evening), a party to celebrate a house sale with an Arabian Nights theme, a staff party, a turning-50-years-old party with a Mexican theme, an herbal festival, a nurses' retreat, a teachers' retreat, and on and on. (I will write more about this later.)

So far, I have only been invited to be part of two weddings, but they have been memorable events for me. The much smaller of the two marriages took place at a beautiful guest house owned by a friend of mine. A couple in their twenties decided to get married there one weekend. I was invited to give them a tea leaf reading.

Whenever I tell this story, I almost always get a response from someone, including my son, Luke, that goes something like this: "Shouldn't they have got the reading before they decided to get married?"

The assumption always seems to be that the only reason a couple would get a reading would be to find out if they would be a good match for a successful marriage.

"No," I respond to this assumption. "I think they know they love each other and want to be married, but they are curious to know how their lives will unfold together."

I got right into the spirit of being part of the wedding even though I have never been married and do not really believe in marriage, although I believe in people being in couples when their lives are being enriched by each other.

In a way, I had no choice but to participate in this one to the best of my abilities. My friend phoned me a couple of days before the event to ask me if I would "pinch hit" as one of the witnesses. It seems the husband of the marriage commissioner was unable to be there to stand up for the couple.

"Okay," I said.

I needed a ride to my friend's guest house, and I ended up being chauffeured there by a client (who always owed me money so did not mind doing these kinds of favours for me) in his older model Cadillac.

When I got to the guest house, I was assigned another duty: to keep the videotape camera directed towards the young couple while the short ceremony was performed. This was to show their families, the bride explained. I am not sure if they had told their families that they were getting married that weekend, but I guess having a videotape would be proof, as well as help make amends if any of the relatives were hurt by not being invited to be there.

The bride was wearing a beautiful, lacy, off-white dress that looked very much like a traditional bridesmaid's dress. She confided that she bought it at a second-hand store. The groom was in a rented tuxedo. Both opted to stand in front of the marriage commissioner in bare feet.

After the ceremony, I gave them a reading. I remember telling them information about how their university experiences would develop into careers. She was training to be a teacher, and he, I think, an accountant. The fact that they were university students explained why they did not want a big, expensive wedding.

They cracked open a bottle of champagne, and later, my friend invited me for dinner. The day had all the elements of a wedding, minus a lot of people.

Recently, I was invited to do readings at a wedding planned by a good friend of the groom. He said he often found weddings to be boring, and he was determined that this one would be anything but. He had invited fire eaters, jugglers, Buddhist monks, and me. I was assigned to do readings for the guests in a tent as the whole event was outside. (I will add more about this in my chapter about parties.)

"Sort of a circus," I told a friend.

"That makes sense," replied my friend, who had gone through a very bad marriage and had lived to tell the tale. "Marriage is a circus."

****

I often tell clients things that will make a big difference in their lives if they come true. On the other hand, if they do not come true, then I might be considered a charlatan at worst, or at least, they would think I am incompetent and might not return to me for a reading.

I know it is a risk to mention these things that seem so totally unlikely, but I believe Higher Power gives me these messages to pass on, and so I believe it would be dishonest not to pass them on. I believe I always see the pictures accurately, but sometimes I do misinterpret what I am seeing.

Take one client, whom I will call Sophia. She saw me several times over a span of many years. When I first saw her, she was married to a man and had small children. Many things I told her came to pass.

But I guess there was one prophecy that bothered her because it was such an important one. I told her that she was going to adopt a girl, and I described her as having shoulder length brown hair.

Time went by and it must have been obvious for her that this did not happen. After all, one knows when one adopts a child. That is a big thing in a person's life and maybe something even more meaningful for Sophia because she was adopted herself.

In the meantime, Sophia met a woman and they fell in love. They had been living together for two years when she came to me for a reading one day. "You know," she said, "I think it is Georgia (her female partner) that you were talking about when you said I was going to adopt a girl. She has the same features that you described to me in that reading when you told me I would adopt someone, and she is very small."

"So she probably looked like a little girl when I saw her in my mind's eye," I said.

Also, because Sophia was married to a man for so many years, the Universe was showing me something that intellectually I never would have expected—that Sophia would enter a lesbian relationship.

We both nodded and smiled in delight with how the Universe works or, rather, with how we can misinterpret its messages.

****

Sometimes, love is dead. The only thing that the Universe can suggest, through my intuition, is that it should be buried ASAP so the seeker can get on with his or her life minus the hollowness of living with someone you no longer love.

One woman, who came to me to ask about her marriage, had the dead love of her relationship in her eyes.

"What, specifically, do you want to know about your marriage?" I asked, knowing it was no good for her if we beat around the bush.

"Will it ever work?" she asked, her face sad and her shoulders slumped.

I closed my eyes to channel. I saw nothing there. "No, there is nothing there," I said. "You have many years left in your life still. You should leave the marriage and be happy."

"That's what my children say," she said. "You are right. There is nothing there."

On the same day, a man came to me with the same kind of question: "Should I end my relationship?"

I channelled and saw a very cold, repressed woman. "Yes, you should," I said.

It was as if I had told him that he had won the lottery. He was excitedly animated in his joy. He eagerly looked forward to changing his career as well. Unlike the woman with the dead eyes, he was wholeheartedly embracing change in his life.

I also picked up that he was actually gay, so maybe another part of the change that was coming for him was coming out as his true self.

****

Of course, there is the person who comes for a reading because s/he believes s/he loves someone else. Yvanna has come often for readings. The man she is in love with has made it clear that he does not want her in his life.

Although she never seems even to see the two of them together, she is in love with this man because, in my intuitive opinion, he made her realize how companionable a man can be to a woman. In that way, he woke her up to how lacking her own husband is as a good companion.

Her husband provides her with everything, including good financial support, but not with this. He also likes to control how she is. Being "in love" with this other man makes Yvanna go and get a tattoo because she wants to, even if her husband does not want her to have one. She sees that she is separate from her husband, has needs, and is realizing them.

I told Yvanna about my once moving to a community because (or so I thought) I was to be with a man there. Later, an intuitive woman told me he was only the "sugar" to get me to move and to have a better life, including following my passion.

Yvanna does not buy it (not yet anyway) that the man she is enamoured with is merely a means to an end: being fulfilled in her own life. Sometimes, when I do a reading, the client wants to see only so far because s/he is hung up on part of the process that is helping them transition into a new life. In Yvanna's case, it will be life without a controlling husband. She refuses to see yet that, some day, the man she is in "love" with will be nothing but a happy memory, if that.

****

I remember Renee being so heartbroken about the possibility of moving from one community to another. The schooling prospect for her daughter was better in the community she was thinking of moving to.

I intuited that it would be a good move for both of them. I saw she would get into a relationship with a man, and I even saw that his name would be Abby. (It is quite unusual for me to see the name of a person who is going to be someone's lover or influential in another way in someone's life.) I saw everything would go well.

"Then, why do I feel so sad?" she asked, more than once.

I think I responded with something a bit deep like, "It is natural to grieve when you leave a place you enjoyed living in."

Things did work out in a lot of ways for Renee. She did meet Abby. They had a relationship for several years, which went sort of crazy (mostly on his part) at the end, but I think it did help settle Renee into her new community in a lot of ways. Former lovers and family members followed her to her new place of residence.

This, of course, is another example of why I need to stick with what I intuit when I give a reading and not be swayed by someone's sadness.

****

Then there was Mila. She was a great mother and a great partner to her husband. She also was keen on moving ahead in her work life. Then, I stumbled upon the fact that she was filled with fear that she would do what her mother did.

What did her mother do?

Her mother had an affair.

This bright, lovely woman thought that she would one day throw away the basically good life that she had.

One of the things I saw was that she should work this fear through with a therapist. I seldom see this, as I think, often, people come to psychics because they have reached a dead end with a counselor or to supplement their time in therapy. In this case, I saw she needed to talk it out in maybe six sessions.

****

I try to keep tissues on hand because people often shed tears during a reading with me. Ninety-nine percent of the time, it is not a bad thing. Sometimes, it is the first chance they have had to stop "running," sit down, and tell someone about the problem that has been bothering them for, often, a very long time.

Lovey was one of these. She was having an affair, and what was eating her up on the inside was the guilt—but probably more so that she had not shared what she was doing with any of her friends, even though, at least once a year, Lovey went on a retreat weekend with those very friends. She was with those friends when she first came for a reading from me.

I saw that the affair was not the problem. "What kind of a wench is this tea leaf reader?" you might be asking.

Not a wench, but someone who listens to her intuition.

I channelled the information that the problem was her marriage, and the affair was helping her to go on. Also, the man with whom she was having the affair was the one who she should be with in a fulltime relationship.

This is why it is important for the reader to use her intuition and not fall back on some personal moral or ethical code that does not work for everyone and differs from culture to culture. Using my intuition means I will tell each client what is right for that particular individual.

A year later, Lovey came back with her group of friends. She told me that, immediately after she got the reading from me the year before, the man she was having an affair with was confronted by his wife. He did not deny it but saw it as an opportunity to change his life for the better.

Lovey said, since then, the relationship between the two of them had expanded in wonderful ways. She had told her husband. They were in separate bedrooms and waiting for their house to sell before going on with their lives in different directions. She said this also was giving their teenage daughters a chance to get adjusted to the fact that their parents would be getting a divorce.

In the course of the year, Lovey had been open about her situation with her friends. What did she learn?

"Everyone has affairs," she said.

****

I will conclude this chapter by saying that, as long as people want to be in love or are in love, psychics will continue to get work giving them readings.

I feel warmth in my heart when I remember doing a reading for Stella one brilliantly bright sunny day. "You will meet someone new to have a love relationship with," I remember telling her.

Quite a while later, her daughter told me that Stella had, in fact, met someone.

She was more than eighty years old.

On the other hand, one woman (I will call her Maggie), during a reading, told me that she enjoyed her solitude. Maggie is the only one I recall saying this to me. I wonder if others would, too, if we did not live in such a couples-addicted society. Personally, I agree that being alone does not necessarily mean being lonely for a partner. I know I am whole within myself whether I am alone or in a relationship.

Chapter Six

Reading for the Rich and Famous

I would not have recognized actress Goldie Hawn if I had not been told by Jackie, who was working at the market where I was tea leaf reading one summer, that it was she who wanted to get a tea leaf reading from me.

Jackie pulled me into the entranceway of a business that bordered the edge of the market and pushed me towards a woman. She was about five feet eight inches, with a white peaked cap pulled down over her long, messy, curly, blonde hair. She wore a baggy shirt and jeans. Her disguise was a good one. I never would have picked her out in a crowd.

"Oh, hello," I said. "I am the tea leaf reader." We shook hands. "Would you like a tea leaf reading?" (I am always super composed when I am nervous.)

"Yes, I would," she said, "but let's try not to make a big deal about it." Okay. I got it. She did not want to draw any attention to herself that might result in being mobbed.

I went to heat some water and to tell a friend, who was waiting for a reading, that he would have to wait. When I told him why and that he needed to keep this confidential, he slipped me a bar of his soap from off the stall where he was selling it. "Give this to her for me," he said.

I did and Goldie giggled. She was genuinely flattered. Her laughter and the way she was taking everything in around her was just the way she always was in her comedic movies. She was a delight.

She was also diplomatic, I soon learned. "My son wants to have a reading," she said.

"So, you don't want a reading?" I asked. I only wanted to clarify how many cups of tea I should bring in.

"I want one," she said carefully, "but first things first." She looked at a tall young man who had a carbon copy Kurt Russell (his father) face and Goldie's blonde hair.

Being intuitive definitely has its advantages. Right away, I got that she is a good mother and likes to step aside (and take her fame with her) so her children can enjoy their lives. In fact, I later was told that she had moved her film studio to a different city because her son was going to play hockey at the university there.

I read his cup and I saw that he was going to spend time playing hockey in Europe, and so on, and so forth. But what he really wanted to know was what every seventeen-year-old boy would want to know if he had just moved to a new town. "Will I keep on dating my girlfriend in L.A.?" he asked.

It did not look good. The fickle, stupid hearts of some teenage girls is all I have to say.

The reading over, mother and son found each other. Goldie had to go. She did not offer to pay for the reading, and I could not work up the courage to ask for money. This rarely happens with me, and it is embarrassing to confess this, but seeing as these are my confessions, I feel I have to confess.

Not to worry. I decided I would get my money's worth in publicity and called the local paper about the events of the afternoon. I have mentioned it on posters and in other publicity ever since. Some people have been hooked into getting readings from me because, initially, they have wanted to find out from me what Goldie Hawn is really like. She is terrific and has the personality and exuberance of a hummingbird.

Someone came for a reading with me on the day after I met Goldie. She said she and her girlfriend had been walking by and had spotted Kurt Russell in the area also. Apparently, her friend had sort of gasped or panted, but she explained that, as a flight attendant herself, she was much too savvy to do such a thing, and her friend had embarrassed her.

I am no groupie myself, but I remember Goldie on the *Laugh In* television show and in her stellar roles in *Butterflies are Free* and *Cactus Flower,* so it was, like I say, a blast to meet her.

In the end, she indirectly got her monies worth from me in turn. I rented every single movie I could find her in at the local video store, and even some starring her daughter, Kate Hudson.

A few days later, the shop owner from whom I rented my market space called me in a rage. Apparently, Goldie Hawn was her regular customer, and the shop owner felt I had somehow disturbed her. She had heard that I had made a deal with Goldie to give her a free tea leaf reading in exchange for getting a photograph with her. This was untrue, of course.

No wonder the tabloids do such a booming business. This just gives me a small hint as to what it must be like to be famous.

****

Reading Bill Richardson's tea cup was a great experience. For those of you who do not know, he is a long time CBC Radio personality.

One afternoon, I was listening to *Richardson's Roundup,* when someone called in with a story about tea leaf reading. In response to this, Bill asked the listeners to phone in with stories on this topic.

I looked at the guy I was dating at the time. "I think the Universe has just manifested an opportunity for me," I said. I called and left a message: "I don't want to tell you a story about tea leaf reading, but if you like, I can give you one because I am a tea leaf reader."

I must have been sounding particularly flirtatious that day or Bill was feeling particularly gay (which he is, of course, and is very "out" about it), because next day, I received a return message from him that went something like this:

"Were you meaning that you wanted to give me a reading on a … er … social level or on a … er … professional …I mean, I find the idea of doing it on the air really intriguing."

I quickly called back. "Oh, yes, yes, yes. I phoned with the intent of doing it as part of your radio program."

The next day, we taped the reading. As with all my long distance readings, I drank the cup of tea for Bill. He called me at a time we had agreed upon, and then I did the reading in the same way I would if he had been sitting with me.

Of course, Bill's cup was filled with stuff about media networks trying to entice him over to them, him being a celebrity tour guide in the summer, him writing another book. I was actually seeing all those things, but it would have been easy for Bill to think I was just making these things up based on what I knew about him from listening to him on the radio.

Then, he asked me about his dogs. Immediately, this feeling of indignity welled up in me, starting from the pit of my stomach. "Well, the bigger dog is bullying the smaller one," I said. I even remember putting my hands on my hips as I told him this. I was so annoyed by the big dog's misbehaviour.

"You are dead on," Bill responded. "The bigger one starts howling at four every morning."

Always one to champion the underdog (and this time I was doing it literally), I told Bill, "You really should get the bigger dog into obedience school."

"Or have her mouth wired shut," Bill responded in exasperation and with his typical wry wit.

The next day, when I got home in the early afternoon, I checked my voicemail. Even though the program had not yet aired in my part of the country, I already had messages from people in Toronto who wanted a reading. They called continuously for the whole month of November, from almost every Canadian province and from Upstate New York. Some continued to be my clients for several years.

The CBC Radio people put my phone number on their website. That is all it took.

The readings I did at that time are a good cross section of the type of readings I do all the time. I remember encouraging one caller to go and work with a shaman in Haida Gwai (the Queen Charlottes). Another woman in small town Alberta had been fired from her job and was wondering what her prospects in the future would be. Another in Prince Edward Island phoned and made an appointment with me during a major power outage in her province. (Maybe she thought it was a sign that she should get a reading.) There was the woman in the Rocky Mountains who was experiencing a crisis because her partner, who was a mountain climbing guide, had seriously injured himself. She also had an alcoholic brother who gave her lots of concern. Another in Ontario was considering a work change to landscaping. I advised her about how that would come about for her.

One of the New York State clients was an elderly woman I'll call Marie, who wondered if she would ever get up to Montreal to study French. I saw that she was to embark on a journey over three mountains. A mountain, when I see it in someone's cup, usually means a challenge. Then, I look at how difficult the challenge will be for them to surmount by seeing how steep, rounded, or jagged the mountain is. Her daughter, who also became a client, told me Marie had triple heart bypass surgery that year in Florida, and she probably literally went over three mountains to get to the hospital where the surgery was done. This is often how images in the cup work. They are literal as well as symbolic of something that will happen.

****

It was because of a close friend of mine that I got to read Charlotte Diamond's tea leaves. My friend had worked for her in the past, and so Charlotte came to do a performance in our home town.

After the performance, my friend served sushi at her home for a small group of us. I cannot remember, but I think Charlotte had not had a tea leaf reading before, or not for a while anyway.

We went up into my friend's bedroom suite, where I read Charlotte's leaves. It was great to meet her because, when my son, Luke, was small, I remember borrowing one of her song cassettes from the corner library and playing it over and over again for my little one.

I saw in Charlotte's cup that she was torn between moving her career to an even higher level (she was world famous by this time and, I think, had just got back from performing in Costa Rica or was just on her way there) or spending more time with her family. Again, it came home for me: people have the same kind of challenges in their lives whether they are famous or not. Charlotte's challenge is the challenge of so many career women.

I remember seeing an important event Charlotte would participate in with many other international stars that was to be held in Washington, D.C. Probably, what I was seeing was an event in opposition to the Iraqi war.

At the after-concert gathering, there was another musician who was probably technically superior to Charlotte, but it was easy to see why the children's performer is much better known. She has an energy that is contagious. She is interested in everything, including turning over every stone to broaden her career. She is a very appealing personality. This is probably what people mean when they say someone has stage presence.

****

I think I had read Andrea Collins' tea leaves a couple of times before I realized who she was. (No, my intuition does not flash information to me about who someone is. In fact, I am sure my spirit guides do not care whether someone on the earth plane is famous or not.) She is the ex-wife of super rock star Phil Collins. But who she really was, was a small blonde woman with a British accent who seemed a bit down about her life. Someone in the press once described her as diminutive. I think our expectations are warped. We expect the famous to be larger than life. In my experience, they often appear smaller than they do on television, for example.

One thing I know for sure: she did not come across as a famous person. But what are famous people supposed to be like? And of course, technically, she was not a famous person. She just had been married to a famous person. In fact, as I got to know her over time, it seemed that she actually had given up her own chance to be famous in exchange for marrying someone famous.

She met Phil Collins at a London art school, where, as a teenager, she got the opportunity to act in a play with Vanessa Redgrave in the West End theatre district. At one point, she was one of two long-blonde-haired, mini-skirted "birds" in a white band, in which Phil was involved, that played Motown music.

It seemed one of the reasons the marriage finally broke up was due to Andrea's boredom in going with Genesis in one limousine after another to one stadium after another to one hotel room after another. She as well did not think taking children on the road was a good idea.

The questions she asked during readings were the usual relationship questions, and I remember her asking about whether she should sell her horse. I cannot think of anything out of the ordinary about the readings I gave her. Having connections with fame does not mean a person is out of the ordinary or unusual in any way, really.

It is just that the mass media, particularly the tabloid press and entertainment shows, has a way of magnifying everything that famous people do. A good example of this is when a Canadian Press journalist called me when I was working as a reporter on the local newspaper during a protest against tree clear-cutting in the area.

"Is it true that Andrea Collins has shaved her head and chained herself to a logging truck?" was the question I was asked.

I put my hand over the phone mouthpiece. "Hey," I yelled across the newsroom. "Has anyone seen Andrea Collins over the weekend?"

"Yeah," someone responded.

"Was her head shaved?" I asked, feeling sure that it was not.

"No," was my verification.

Andrea and I had a good laugh over that one.

****

Quite a few professionals in many different fields have come to me for readings, but seldom have politicians. Maybe they believe that making laws involves linear thinking and has nothing to do with the intuition or with seeking intuitive guidance. But surely, making political decisions are not always black and white. For the shades of grey in life, we often need to go to our intuition.

Jean Crowder, the Member of Parliament for Nanaimo-Cowichan on Vancouver Island (as I am writing this), got a reading from me once when I did readings at the home of a leader in the First Nations community. With her ties to this community, it did not surprise me when I later found out she was appointed as NDP Critic for Aboriginal Affairs.

I do not remember what I told her during the reading, but I do remember how she really listened to what I had to say. She smiled with open interest.

Years earlier, I was asked by the NDP to consider running for their party on a municipal level. Whenever I told anyone about this, I always added, "I should have said I don't want to be a politician, but I would like to be a spiritual advisor to politicians."

I have long thought that, if elected politicians were asked to close their eyes and meditate before making governmental decisions, we would live in a much more peaceful and harmonious society. I think politicians seeking intuitive guidance would help as well.

It is well known that Prime Minister William Lyon Mackenzie King sought guidance through intuitive mediumship. He did not do any worse as a leader than the prime ministers who did not seek this guidance, and many would say that he did much better.

In *The Oxford Companion to Canadian History,* H. Blair Neatby writes that it was only after King's death that "Canadians learned that this apparently dull man believed in the immanence of the spirit world. King needed emotional support. When he could not get it from the living, he turned to the dead. The assurance he found there had given him the strength to survive the stress of his lengthy political career."[2] (King was prime minister for 22 years.)

****

There are also those who are rich but want to totally shy away from any fame that might come with it. I once went on a rather madcap evening of tea leaf readings at a town a ferry ride away from where I was living. I was without a car for a while so had to be picked up by one of the people that were getting a reading at the party.

The last reading I gave that night was for a man whom I will call Will. He had a British accent, but I picked up on his energy and found him very warm with a great sense of humour.

At one point, as an aside, I said to him, "I don't want to sound stereotypical, but you seem a bit unusual for a Brit."

"Oh," he said, "I am a total eccentric."

" You mean, for a person of British background?" I asked.

"For someone of any background," he said. "Like, right now, I am wearing my pajamas ... I often go out in the evening to get milk or something, and I don't see why I should have to get dressed for

---

[2] Hallowell, *The Oxford Companion to Canadian History,* 337.0l.

it." Will did have his jacket on over top, so I would not have noticed he had on his pajamas if he had not pointed it out.

One of the messages I had for him was that he would be connected to a film or some kind of other media project on a behind-the-scenes basis. When he drove me back to the ferry in his rebuilt jaguar, he explained to me that he had had wealth, lost it, and then gained it back again three times in his life. "At Christmas, I always give money to working people," Will said. "They might be single working people or couples, but I always do it anonymously. I learned early on that drawing publicity to yourself as a wealthy person creates all kinds of problems." So, he made the point that I was right about him doing something behind the scenes.

He told me that he came from a working class background in Britain and did not realize that he was poor until he came to North America. He also told me something else that people might not expect from the wealthy. "I stayed in a marriage for twenty-four years," he said. "It was bad for twenty-three and a half years. My wife was an alcoholic, but I stayed in it until my youngest child turned eighteen."

I saw in the reading that the woman he was dating at that point was going one way, and he was going in the exact opposite direction. "She's driven," he said. "I am not going to put up with that anymore."

Will also said he gave his children really nice cars as graduation gifts but that he was not going to leave them money in his will. He wanted them to make their own way through life.

In a lot of ways, he seemed more exceptional than any of the famous people that I did readings for. He had realized that how we live our lives makes us filled with abundance or not. Having lots of money means very little if relationships and day-to-day life are not providing happiness.

I often have had very little money, but my philosophy is very similar. At a metaphysical shop where I do readings, I picked up a square plaque with a Thoreau quote on it. I have it hanging over the table in my living room where I display my tea cups. It says:

"Wealth is the ability to fully experience life." And I would also like to add that being famous does not mean you experience life more fully or better than anyone else does.

So, how did I get this opinion? Well, I occasionally have done readings for the rich and famous, but also, to a lesser degree, I am famous, too.

There are, of course, positives. Opportunities sometimes come my way because I am quite well known (at least in the part of the world in which I am based). This is in combination with the fact that I am quite good at what I do.

People are often very complimentary and want to help me to get ahead, to get out there. If someone has experienced receiving a good reading from me, then that person wants to share me with his or her friends. Because of this, I have been able to do readings in beautiful heritage homes and in an art gallery. Tea shops have given me tea to use at events, such as a tea festival. Others offer me a place in their home and even a bed to sleep in. Meals, from barbequed salmon—with all the trimmings and topped up with cheesecake dessert and wine—to finger food have been served to me. Many want me to make more money. People give me feedback about how my readings affect their lives in a positive way.

On the other side of things, there is also the jealousy factor, when things are going well, and the competitive factor from some psychics. I personally have come to agree with Deepak Chopra. He writes in his book *Creating Affluence: Wealth Consciousness in the Field of all Possibilities* that we should exult "in the success of others, especially your competitors and those who consider themselves your enemies. Your competitors and enemies will become your helpers when you exult in their success."[3]

I truly have come to enjoy, for example, doing trades with other psychics for readings. I would not even *want* to miss out on this marvelous connecting with my colleagues, or as Thea Trussler, a

---

[3] Chopra, Creating Affluence: Wealth Consciousness in the Field of All Possibilities, 31.

Tarot reader, calls them, "our tribe." Often, we do our work alone, so it is nice to put jealousy and competitiveness aside and celebrate how wonderful we and our profession are.

Another thing that has happened to me is what I will call being vulnerable to needy people. The fact that I am good at what I do and exude that energy, as well as my being quite well-known, mean that a handful of people at any given time will phone me constantly to ask me the same questions that I already answered for them. Some try to make me feel that it is my duty to give them readings at any time of day or night. Others are drama queens who hint at doing or even threaten to do something harmful to themselves if I do not drop everything to give them attention. Some are master manipulators. All of them are insecure. They have a bottomless-well effect on me: the more I give to them, the more they want. They are energy drainers and sometimes make me quite angry and frustrated. I have given them really thorough readings and lots of attention, but still they want more.

I am sure that people who are more famous than I am really struggle with needy people trying to get something out of them, along with the lack of privacy, as well as with the jealousy and competitiveness. What outweighs all of this is that I have met many more incredible people through doing readings than the few who are needy. Actually, I should say they are incredible spirits because I always connect with their spirits or the best part of who they are when I use my psychic skills.

As well, the spiritual growth for me has contributed to my pleasure in life to a degree that is totally beyond measure or the putting of a value on it.

****

There are others to whom I have given readings who also are famous or accomplished in their own circles but are not household names.

There is the broadcaster who feared she would be laid off when national cuts were made. I said, "No, but you will be expected to do more work for less money." I was right. When she phoned with this news, I asked, jokingly, "Who's your favourite psychic?"

She wanted to know about a meeting in which she wanted to express the things that needed to change for her in the workplace in order to adhere with government legislation. "The meeting will not happen," I said. She phoned in a couple of weeks to say the meeting did not happen because she had been too sick to go to work.

There was the wife of a famous musician who came to me because she was psychologically feeling trapped. Going back to him meant being "soul dead," but there were the children to think of. Going forward meant no money, and if she hired a lawyer to get what was totally hers under law and morally, he threatened immediate divorce, while mentally abusing her into thinking that she was crazy.

There were the filmmakers from Hollywood, but I did not recognize them because they were not the on-screen stars who virtually everyone recognizes.

The women who get the delicious cakes and other foods ready for the covers of the glossy magazines found near the checkout lines at supermarkets were also clients. They were celebrating the work their secretary had done for them by spending a week a couple of states north of California in a vacation rental. I was the entertainment.

A baroque singer who had sung her way around the world many times is another who got a reading from me. I admitted to her that I was ignorant as to who she was. She was gracious.

From these experiences, I am not prepared to say that I would never want to be as famous or rich as the really rich and famous. What I am prepared to say is that problems, and getting good help to overcome those problems, are just as rampant among these people as they are for anyone in any other segment of society.

Chapter Seven

Making it Work

Fairly often, people come to me to explore an aspect of work. It can be how to get the job they want, how to get out of the job they hate, which career to go into, or how to find out what is their passion and how they can go about living or working at their passion.

Listening to my own intuition in relation to work has really made me change my attitude towards work. My intuition in this area, as it has done in many other areas, has made me realize that many rules, especially societal rules, often need to be broken.

Carolyn Myss, the medical intuitive, in her book *Anatomy of Spirit*, highlights how people can literally become seriously ill because they hate an aspect of the life they are living. She points out that this can include hating their work. Just quitting the work they hate can make them well. On the other hand, refusing to change one's work, like the dentist Myss describes who feels he must provide a high level of financial stability for his family, can hasten someone's death.

When I read about this man, I wondered if he had never considered that his family might have preferred him being alive for them as opposed to making their lives so financially secure. Ironic, isn't it?

I saw the irony, too, when I did a couple of readings for a client I will call Iris. She admitted to me that she hated her job. Every morning, she said, she felt anxious just at the thought of going to work.

Her place of work was filled to the brim with office politics. Iris had told a fellow worker that she was allergic to the perfume that the individual wore. Somehow, it was interpreted as being a racial putdown. Iris was warned that she was, under no circumstances, to talk to the individual who wore the perfume.

Every workday, Iris went into her office and waited for the "shoe to drop." She was concerned each day that she was going to be fired. She had witnessed many other unfair firings in her workplace.

Iris had developed cancer on her lip. It was easy for me to intuitively interpret that she was getting sick because she had been silenced at work. She could not move her lips. She could not speak. She had been silenced.

I told her that she should not be afraid of being fired. If she spoke her truth and lost her job, she would get a cash settlement and would be able to go on unemployment insurance for a year. Then, she could return to the intentional community in Europe to which she was yearning to return and where, in the past, she had always been able to get work even when many others could not.

So, what she thought was the worst scenario for her—to lose her job—could turn out to be the best scenario for her. The Universe often closes a door in one area of a person's life so another door can be opened and, when entered, present us with a better life.

I know this from my own experience. I was living in a beautiful place, but there was little work of any kind to be had there. Being self-employed, as I am as an intuitive, can also be quite a challenge.

So, I kept thinking I needed a part-time paycheck. I got one job after the other that I never would have taken if I had been living anywhere else. One of the jobs was sorting mail and the other one was cleaning in a hotel. With both of these jobs, I was, to my humiliation, basically fired.

Then, the most interesting thing happened. My income started to increase and I was able to travel (which I love) a lot again. The Universe was sending me a strong message: do not hang on to work that you hate doing; go with your tea leaf reading, which is your passion, and you will make more money and enjoy life more.

We live in a society that says we need to have a pay cheque in order to survive financially, especially if we are single women. When we listen to our spirit guides, we will find out that this is not necessarily so.

There are those, of course, who say that none of us who are doing spiritual work, such as tea leaf readings, should get paid because it is channelled through from Higher Power and people should not have to pay for this information.

When a friend disclosed to me recently her indecisiveness about making money from doing readings because of this reason, Spirit moved me very quickly to respond. "Do you think we should only get paid for work that we hate doing instead of getting paid for following our passion?" I asked.

Sometimes, I think we do believe that we do not deserve to be paid for work that we love doing. Sometimes, I think people do not see the work of a psychic as being real work. I am doing what I can to change these false notions.

****

Of course, getting to do the work we feel passionate about can mean deciding to say "yes" to the Universe and then taking the steps needed to get it.

I remember one young woman, Elona, who came to get a reading. She was broke but wanted to get a degree in environmental studies. The school she wanted to attend was difficult to get into, but the administration had accepted her.

What made the whole thing tricky was that she needed money and wanted to approach her grandfather to give her the money that she needed. He was quite conservative, and Elona thought he would not necessarily be impressed by what she wanted to do.

I channelled into her grandfather's consciousness and gave her the information on how he would respond to her request. It was like strategizing on how to win a debate with her grandfather by tuning in to how he would respond to it.

There was also another client named Cardamon who was passionate about working with plants. She did not know whether to go into an apprenticeship program to learn more about herbal remedies or to get her master's degree in botany.

I saw that she could have both. So, it was just a matter of which one she should go into first. Intuitively, I saw that she should apprenticeship first and then get her master's degree. A year later, she saw me one day as I was getting into my car.

"You know, I did exactly what you intuited because the courses I needed to work on for the master's degree turned out not to be available for me to take," she said.

In both of these cases, I took on the role of a guidance counselor but went a step further by using my intuition to help solve a dilemma for each young woman.

****

One of the work related issues on which I have done divination involves the legal case of Equal Pay for Work of Equal Value. Three decades ago, when I was employed and very active in the feminist community, this concept made perfect sense. If a woman works at a job that is valued as equal to one that a man holds, then she should be paid the same as the man. This would rid the world of low paying job ghettos for women.

In the Canadian federal government, public service unions have applied to make this possible based on government legislation that makes this legal. In fact, they have applied to make it retroactive back to the date when the law was passed.

When I first started doing readings fourteen years ago (at time of writing), one of my first clients was someone who worked as a cleric in a federal penitentiary. She asked me at that time when things would be settled regarding the Equal Pay for Work of Equal Value case.

In the last couple of years, I have done readings several times for a client who also wants to know when a settlement will take place. She works in the health care sector, evaluating claims.

My point here is that, in thirteen years, thousands and thousands of women across Canada have been waiting for a substantial settlement that the federal government does not want to pay.

My more recent client took me out for dinner when the court finally ruled in favour of the workers. Meanwhile, Prime Minister Stephen Harper, a Conservative Party member and an economist, put forward legislation to renege on the Equal Pay for Work of Equal Value law. A coalition of the other federal parties won a non-confidence vote against Harper's government based on this and other reasons. So, to date, this law is still valid. However, a lawyer sitting on a federal government commission ruled that there should be no retroactive pay to the federal employees affected.

When clients ask me about something like this, I channel the answers. The recent client was very active in planning strategy on this issue, so I tried my best to supply her with information on this. I have answered questions on how large the settlement will be, when it will be made, when and if to go talk to the media, and even how to deal with her coworkers. I did say that the workers would win, and technically they have.

If I had been asked, "Will the money be forthcoming when the workers win the case," I probably would have seen that it would not be awarded right away. I suppose my point here, in a roundabout way, is that when dealing with government officials and any other entity that is a "quick change artist" and a master in manipulation, the more specific the question, the more accurate the channelled answer will be.

On the other hand, sometimes I seem to telepathically tap into other people's consciousness when I am asked something by a client. For example, when Arlene asks me if she will get contract work in northern Canada, I sometimes channel a "maybe or maybe not." It seems I am intuitively picking up on the boss' indecision as to whether there will be work or not.

Although it is not paid work, some people spend a lot of time working for social causes that they believe are important. Arthur is one client who has done a lot of work in the area of how technology can be hazardous to our health by causing cancer and other illness. Many times, I have worked with him on providing information as to how large corporations would infiltrate their technology into communities that do not want them. I am able to see the landscape around the area and the geographical location where they are going to install their equipment. Also, I can outline arguments to use against these people—at public meetings, for example.

When Arthur wanted his political party to adopt policy against technological infiltration, I did work with him on how to go about doing this. I could see that he needed to set up an information table at the party's convention and to get a wide range of people, with different ideas and beliefs, on a committee to hash out what the actual policy should be.

****

Then there was someone who I will call Geneva who was older and had been working as a teacher for many years. She had gone down to halftime because there were other things that she still wanted to do in her life.

One of the things she thought would be fulfilling for her to do was to choreograph a dance performance that would feature her daughter, who was a professional dancer.

I saw that this would not happen. Why? Her daughter would not want to do this with her mother. Geneva, in fact, did not really want to do it either, but she thought she should as a maternal duty.

Another was a fantasy she had about raising goats. I saw that, no, this would not work either because she would need special licenses to do this in the place where she lived. The red tape would take the enjoyment out of keeping the goats.

I saw that, in fact, what she should do was provide private music lessons (this was her specialty) while continuing to work part-time as a teacher.

So, when someone comes to me with questions about their work, in some ways, I almost take on the role of an employment counselor. There is one huge difference, though: I recommend what the person should be doing or not doing by intuiting pictures (almost like a slow moving film), in which I see the client working at a job, and by seeing whether the person is happy and fulfilled or not.

Chapter Eight

For the Long Run

S ome of the persons who come to me for readings come back time and time again. They become special to me—friends. But at the same time, I am doing work for them, trying to help them make sense of what is happening and will happen to them as they grapple with the blueprint the Universe has laid out for them to follow.

In some cases, I can talk to them a bit about my own dreams, challenges, and joys, but the focus must remain, for the most part, on them. Socializing with them is limited at best. They are paying me for my insights. I do not feel that I have to distance myself from their lives like a therapist does, but I do have to remain a bit detached.

With others, friendship takes on equal importance or even more importance than the psychic readings do. Yet, for the most part, I still will be called upon, at least occasionally, to look in the cup, pull a Tarot card, or use my pendulum.

I think people enjoy the mystery of what the psychic does. They do not necessarily want to see that she, too, can have relationship and financial problems and other challenges just like they do. (If they do see this, they might even think that, if I have problems, maybe I am not the best person to go to in order to get insights on their own problems. Of course, this is not true. Often, we can advise others better than we can take or live our own advice.)

Well, in some ways, I do not have that many challenges, of course, because I have listened to the advice that the spirits and God/dess have channelled through me to my clients. I hear the wisdom they have sent my way to pass on to others. I can pretend that, somehow, I am immune to the very advice I give to others, but of course, I am not. I tend to think that no one who is on the physical plane—no matter how spiritually exalted she or he is—can be immune to having problems.

Sometimes, I use my own shortcomings, or my ability to overcome them, as examples that parallel what the client should or should not do.

More of this later, maybe, but right now, I want to introduce you to some of my long-term clients. They are no more amazing than any of the people who come to see me. This work has taught me that each and every being houses an incredible spirit within. With the long-term ones, though, I get to know more of their stories, and my insights are heightened with regard to what might hold them back in life.

****

I will start with Andrew—the bane of my existence at the same time that he is quite a close friend and a remarkable human being. He has had the ability to trigger me emotionally like no other long-term client. Short-term clients do not usually anger or frustrate me. Nor do most of my long-term clients trigger me in this way. But it will be long-term clients that sometimes make me want to shake them and say, "Have you not heard what I have told you? It is the same message time and time again." A therapist told me once that he feels the same and that he literally experienced a shaking once from his sponsor in the Twelve Step Alcoholics Anonymous program. I have to add that I am not perfect, and maybe I need to have more patience with these clients.

I remember that the first time I saw Andrew, I noticed how very attractive he was. Many of my women acquaintances would agree. And he had the whole package that lots of women fantasize about. The Andrew package consisted of a European background, driving a foreign car, being a professional tennis player, and having attended one of the most prestigious American universities. To top it off, he was blonde and well built. He had sort of a Daniel Craig/James Bond look about him although he did not hail from England.

Andrew started to come to me for readings on a regular basis; actually, that is an understatement because he came much more than a regular client. They say people can become addicted to almost anything. Among Andrew's addictions are psychic readings. Besides me, he gets consultations from at least three or four other psychics whenever he can manage to beg, borrow, and occasionally pay for readings. I always insisted that he pay at least something for the readings I gave him. I did this because I could not afford not to. Giving psychic readings is the primary way I make a living. But in addition to this, I thought making him pay helped control his addiction somewhat.

At first, I did my standard tea leaf readings for him. That quickly shifted to doing short channellings for him. His mantra became, "Just five minutes for five dollars." Then, he would end up spending an hour or even more with me. It got so he was always underfoot. He was around just as much as, if not more than, a lover might be in my life. In fact, this was one of my complaints. I knew people were always seeing his foreign car parked outside my place and were drawing their own conclusions. "How will I even attract another man to be in a relationship with if everyone sees your car parked here?" I would ask him. Of course, being the self-absorbed alpha male that he was, Andrew really did not care how he might be interfering in my life.

He often brought his girlfriend with him, but people seeing his car parked at my place did not know this. At one point, even she wondered about our relationship. She arranged to get a tea leaf reading from me, and her first question was why Andrew was spending so much time with me. "It really is nothing to do with me," I responded. "I think he is addicted to getting psychic readings." To her benefit, she accepted my honest answer.

It was not until several years later that I realized something else about my relationship with Andrew. He had moved to California but still kept calling me several times a week. "I think Andrew is in love with me," I mentioned to a friend.

"You think?" my friend responded, indicating that it was obvious to her that he had feelings for me. I think she was right, but also I do not think Andrew knew much about love from the heart because he was in his head so much. (In his head, he had lots of ideas of what love was and who he should be in love with, but these were merely ideas.) I honestly believe he did not realize that he was in love with me.

This was fine with me because I knew anything romantic with him would have been a total disaster.

You might wonder why, then, I would allow him to be so invasive in my life. So have I. I am normally very good with boundaries, especially when it comes to clients. What hooked me into Andrew, at first anyway, was that he was living a very interesting lifestyle—one that only someone as complex as he is could be living. A friend, who is a counselor, says I like eccentrics because I am an eccentric myself. I think she is right. But often, these eccentrics prove way too eccentric, even for me, and part of being eccentric is being an individual who cannot get along well with other people. You march to the beat of your own drum. Also, because I am very intuitive, they start to drain my energy with their intensity.

By way of a bit of a profile sketch of Andrew: when he left the exclusive university he attended, Andrew worked in the stock market and developed his tennis game to professional status. But his rising star crashed when he developed an extreme allergy to the turf or the pesticides in the turf on and around the tennis courts.

Because Andrew had the personality of a bloodhound, having to quit playing tennis was something he was not willing to accept—beautiful women, friends in high places, and oodles of money being among the fringe benefits that he did not want to forfeit.

If he was allergic to something on the tennis courts, well then, there was nothing else to do than to get rid of what he was allergic to on every tennis court around the world. He set up a company, and then decided this would be his ticket to becoming a multi-millionaire or better.

And, of course, my observations told me that Andrew was bright enough and business minded enough to figure out that if he became an environmentalist and persuaded other environmentalists to take this on as a cause, he could get a lot of free labour out of them, at least while setting the business up, and he could have the lion's share of the money invested in the company.

When I and others of his friends confronted him with this, he was quite hurt. I guess, being from a wealthy background, Andrew just a assumed that making a lot of money was his reward for doing anything—his birthright. He was smart enough to figure out how to make a lot of money, so therefore he should.

Having written all of this, I have to say that Andrew changed in many ways over the years I knew him. In some ways, this is what is very nice about having a long-term client. I see transformation happen, and sometimes it is the transformation that I have intuited. I have seen it many times before. Someone, over time, actually becomes better, or else the better part of the person, buried underneath, surfaces and makes the outward part of the person start to transform.

But going back to the earlier years that I knew Andrew, egocentric being his middle name, he did not stop with wanting to make a lot of money. He started thinking about how to round out his life through marriage. Who would be the best type of woman to help him in his career? Sometimes, he thought that woman should be athletic and a massage therapist so she could help him work out and to relax. Other times, he thought a socialite would be his ticket to his potential investors. And who, after all, could be a better hostess?

Often, Andrew thought the chosen woman should be a psychic because, in some ways, we were his most valuable resources. For example, he was always asking me all kinds of questions that could give him an edge in his business dealings, in his many legal wheelings and dealings, and in relation to his tumultuous personal life.

Love did not seem to enter into the marriage equation for Andrew. He certainly did not want to marry someone for love alone. He was after love with benefits.

Andrew also had a variety of health problems because of numerous bizarre accidents. This, like everything else in his life, created drama, the other thing to which Andrew was hopelessly addicted.

Through filing or trying to file lawsuits, Andrew got to know almost every lawyer practicing across the continent. He hounded them in the same way he hounded psychics.

He came to see me one day in a total huff because one head of a large, prestigious law firm had told him, in no uncertain terms, to cease and desist contacting his staff. He had harassed every lawyer in the firm in the hopes of getting free legal advice.

We spent hours and hours going over names of lawyers and which ones would be most suitable for him. This was fun because I found I could hone in on the personality traits of people I had never met with surprising accuracy. Andrew often confirmed this for me after he had gone to meet with them. (Even if he had been sleeping in his car the night before—which he often did—he would dress impeccably, looking like he had just stepped off a yacht.)

The other thing I liked about Andrew's legal hassles is that I found I could intuit the political action he might want to take in response to something that had happened to him. I would "get" who he should see and what the content of the letter should be. I have a background as a feminist and social activist, so once again, doing this strategizing was interesting and enjoyable for me.

These experiences make me believe that psychics often build on what they already know, so the larger one's life experience, the better. If I am familiar with a particular lifestyle, then I recognize what I am intuiting about it better.

On the other hand, I find I sometimes see something in someone's cup that I can only describe to them as best I can because I don't know what it is or what to call it. For example, someone may be about to get an unusual job or make unusual art. Like the trapeze artist that came for a reading once. I did not know that was her chosen profession as I did the reading, so I described things and she filled in the gaps. She knew what I was talking about even if I did not. I find I sometimes have to go on faith and have the courage to go ahead with the reading.

But to get back to Andrew's story—he told me that lawyers would often say to him, "Where would you get an idea like that from?" It did not fit in with his Ivy League image. Of course, he never told any of them that he frequented psychics—similar to how some businessmen would not disclose that they have liaisons with call girls. (Not that I want to confuse the two professions.) He never told them, that is, until one of his lawyers decided to interview several of us as possible witnesses to Andrew's declining health in connection with an insurance claim.

The lawyer called us "soothsayers" as a way to gently discredit what we do. But often, what psychics do is calm people down without, it is hoped, saying anything that is dishonest, but just by helping someone see something in a better light. More than one man and many women have cried while I have given them readings. It is usually positive crying; getting out their feelings is a positive experience for them.

But to go on about Andrew: while he was trying to get money from a variety of insurance companies, he would often ask me what certain agents were doing regarding his claims. If he was going to a meeting with lawyers, insurance people, possible investors in his company, possible staff for his company, to meet a woman he wanted to get romantic with, with a bank manager, with a possible sponsor, with someone he wanted to purchase something from (it got to the point where I would not have been surprised if he had asked me if he should cross a particular street), I would be consulted as to how he should handle them.

Some psychics disagree with the idea of channelling information about people who are unaware of the fact that they are being evaluated in this way. I always believe that if Higher Power did not want us to tap into this information, then I would not be able to receive it. In fact, I am sure there is a lot of information that I am unable to tap into as a psychic. When someone comes to me for information, it is like doing a form of research.

If someone came and asked me, for example, the best way to rob a bank, I would not work with them. But criminals rarely, if ever, come for readings from me, and if they do, they are not asking me to help them with illegal activities.

I do remember one time doing a Tarot reading, with a guy who I was dating, that basically indicated he should get out of debt by stealing some felled trees that had been abandoned on property owned by the government. This surprised me, but I thought this was the message I got because it was morally corrupt, on an environmental level, for the government to waste these trees. So the Universe felt that taking the trees and using them was justified. About a year after I did this reading, I heard a news story on the radio that outlined the government's conundrum over what to do with these felled trees. In a way, someone taking the trees would indirectly solve the problem. Sometimes, rules are made to be broken.

To conclude with Andrew, though: you probably are asking yourself right now, why on earth would I put up with him?

Good question.

It started out with the fact that I needed the money. I did earn a couple of thousand dollars from him over the several years we knew each other. Not enough to compensate for all the stress I underwent being associated with him, and often against my will, but it was more than most of the psychics he frequented received. Andrew was very good at working out deals with people.

I knew I was getting ripped off, as I think many psychics do. I was doing the work of a good business consultant, a health and legal expert, and a therapist all rolled into one without being recompensed for it. On the other hand, Andrew had the chance of making millions of dollars based on what I told him.

Of course, there was at least one positive. Getting so much practice in channelling greatly improved my accuracy and my confidence. Working with Andrew was like taking an intensive course in divination. He always promised that, if he made a million dollars, he would set me up in fine style. I am still waiting.

****

Aretha is a small, fairy-like woman for whom I did many readings, and we quickly became close friends. She was quite ill when I first met her, and I really admired how she was determined to get well through alternative health care.

Often, her questions for me were whether a particular alternative health care practitioner was a good one for her to go to for healing. When I said that, "Oh, yes, this person will be wonderful for you to go to," then she thought my readings were great.

But sometimes, I saw that the healer would not do her any good or that to go to that healer at a time when her health was particularly fragile would affect her in a negative or, even, in a very negative way. If she had decided, however, then she would go regardless of what I said. Fears would drive her into thinking, "I should go now while I have the money," and to ignore her instinct or intuition that was saying, "Extreme caution: you will probably get really sick if you do this." (I can understand these fears around money.)

Then, because I am really good friends with Aretha, she would call me daily in her very needy desperation. I know that, often, her life was hovering between life and death. It was exasperating for me, though, when I had intuitively advised her against getting that particular healing. I also knew by then that, in fact, people often do have to decide for themselves whether they want to live or die.

So, if Aretha really wanted to live, then she would not have endangered her life in that kind of way (and this was not the first time that she had done this). In fact, she started to talk with me about feeling that maybe she no longer had the energy to stay alive.

Emotionally, I was grieving because Aretha really is a dear friend to me. But intuitively, I had to tell her the truth. I had to tell her what Higher Power was relaying or channelling through me as a message to her. Of course, she has her choice or free will, but sometimes people take it at great peril to themselves. She was constantly putting herself into crisis.

For many people, I would often intuit that they should take the risk and bring change into their lives. With Aretha, I saw that, health-wise, she often was not ready to change her life, although intellectually, she thought she was ready.

I have learned a lot about how our intelligence, our emotions, and our intuition work. You can be sure of yourself in one of those areas, while in another of the areas, you can be totally unsure—or that part of you even can totally "war" against the part that has decided something.

I am not an astrologer, but I know a bit about how a person's horoscope sign affects that individual. In a rather simplistic, general way, anyone who is an air sign (Libra, Aquarius, or Gemini) will decide or want to decide something by going to his or her head.

Aretha is Libra, so her intelligence often tells her that she will be okay if she goes ahead and does something. And Libras so much want life to be rational, so they will have a tendency to want to go ahead and do something even when their intuition or instincts, if they stopped to listen, would tell them that, emotionally, they were not ready.

Having said all this, Aretha did talk to me about another way of looking at all of this. She said that, in my readings for her, I often picked up clairvoyantly on her fears. So, she felt going ahead and doing something was a way of her overcoming her fears. I am not totally convinced that this was what was going on. I think, sometimes, other fears (e.g. if I don't do this now, I will have no money to do this later) would get in the way of her intuitive or instinct-based fear concerning how it would ill affect her health. She had layers of fears.

****

Another regular client and friend provided me with an interesting lesson when she decided to sell her leaky condominium. When Giselle asked me what month it would sell, I intuited January. "Oh, no," she wailed, "I CAN'T possibly stay here that long."

Not wanting Giselle to be experiencing such agony, I decided to help her sell her condo. Into my consciousness popped a friend named Jeanne, who always seemed to be on the lookout for a condominium for herself or someone in her inner circle of friends.

I phoned Jeanne and left her a message. Shortly afterwards, she called back. "You know what just happened," she said, incredulously. "My friend Jerry and I were just talking about buying a condo together. Then, I checked my messages, and there was your message asking if I was in the market for a condo."

"I always say," I said, half jokingly and half seriously, "that quite soon, we will no longer need phones or the Internet. We will just beam messages to each other when they are relevant. That is how we are evolving intuitively."

Jeanne and her friend bought the condo from Giselle for a good price. It turned out her friend was a handyman, so he was able to make the place comfortable for the two of them. Giselle soon found a warm, dry apartment to live in before winter set in.

When Giselle had time to reflect on what happened, she called me.

"I don't understand why it sold sooner than your prediction of January," she said.

"Well, we intervened," I responded. "We used our free will." Obviously, if the Universe had disagreed with what we were doing, we would have been blocked by a wall rather than having everything fall into place so easily. Giselle did not agree with what the Universe had planned, so we altered it.

****

Over the years, the act of tea leaf reading has evolved for me—or maybe it is my intuition that has expanded because of the tea leaf reading. I now also can do straight channelling—as I mentioned in Andrew's story—Tarot reading, and pendulum work as well. These are excellent tools to use in any way, but I sometimes find them particularly helpful if someone just has one question to ask me or one issue with which they want to be assisted on an intuitive level.

Channelling can be done easily and quickly, in person or over the phone, without having to prepare tea first and so on. It happens quickly because our intuition works quickly. It is the first "flash" that comes to mind. It leaves quickly as well, so we perceive and then have to have confidence (or faith) that it is correct because its message does not hang around, and it does not explain why it is correct either.

Beth, like Andrew, calls me quite regularly to ask for short readings on specific challenges that she experiences while going through her daily life. One day, she left a message on my voicemail. She was clearly agitated because she was going to a job in an isolated part of the world in a few days. She had shipped several pieces of luggage ahead of her and found out that someone had signed for them in a town that was the last stop before they would be transported to her isolated work location. The trouble was, according to the employees there, the luggage was not in the office where it should have arrived before it was to be sent to Beth's work place.

When I received Beth's e-mail, I was just getting ready to leave for the cinema. (The thing about what I do is that I do it at a variety of times in order to suit my clients, but sometimes I desperately need to fit in time off for myself. It is not like working a nine-to-five job.) I really wanted to see a movie playing there, but I could tell from Beth's voice that she was very upset. I had never done this before (and haven't since), but I decided to get in my car and ask the Universe for guidance as I drove to the cinema.

I meditated in my mind as I went. Soon, a visual picture, like a slow-motion movie (as I mentioned earlier, this is often how channelling happens for me), was playing through my mind. I saw Beth's luggage as it was shipped up to the town. Then, I saw it sitting in an office. "Is this the office where it is supposed to be?" I asked the voice that often comes inside my head when I do divination. (Yes, I do hear voices, and I am not mentally unbalanced.)

"No," the answer came to me.

"Where is the luggage then?" I asked.

A moving picture showed me that the luggage was in a different office. I saw someone signing for it, someone who knew it needed to go down to the airport the next day. The person knew this because it was a small town, without a lot of luggage and travelers going through it. So, she knew the luggage belonged to Beth, who was going to the isolated place to work. I saw the luggage being taken to the airport the next day, being on the plane, and ending up where Beth would be going.

I arrived at the theatre a few minutes early for the presentation. I went to a pay phone, called Beth, and outlined what I had seen and been told through my Third Eye. It made sense to her because she knew there was another government office in the same building where she had sent her luggage, and there was a small airport where it would have to go next before being transferred to her job site.

"I'm seeing it will be at the airport tomorrow," I said.

Beth, too, is a Libra and wants the world to be a rational place. It gives her a lot of angst when so many around her seem to refuse to be reasonable. Not surprisingly, I guess, with her reason always dominant in her mind, Beth had difficulty hearing her intuition.

I suggested she take my tea leaf reading workshop. This was one of the reasons why I continued to do it—I did not want people to become dependent on me for intuitive readings. It is much more empowering for them to develop their own intuition.

Beth continued, however, to fret about so many things—the desire to get into a long-term relationship, to buy a home, and so on.

****

When clients (whether they are friends or not) who get readings from me keep on coming back to me and, often, ask about the same issue over and over again, I get frustrated, just as I sometimes get frustrated with myself when I get stuck in some area of my life and even get obsessed with it. This is being in victim mode, and especially, once I become friends with someone, I see that the person has the ability to deal with the issue and, one way or another, move on with her or his life. Often, I have provided them, through my intuition, with a way, and sometimes with more than one option, to move forward. I get frustrated because it seems, somehow, I am not getting through to them, and sometimes, it even seems that they want to stay in victim mode. This dependency on me is not good for them or for me.

Like Barbie, who was always having issues with her neighbours but wanted to continue to do battle with them, even after the condominium board asked those very neighbours if they wanted to move and they concurred. She did not take one moment out to celebrate or to thank the Universe for this positive turn of events.

Or like Lita, who was in her 30s and had never been in a relationship, but who would always intellectualize her way out of having a relationship or keep things safe by having emotional relationships with married men. She also was in contact with her father on a weekly basis, who was—guess what—the source of her being stuck in her place of having emotional relationships with men who could never be totally there for her.

Or like Valise, who had obsessive-compulsive disorder (OCD) and was obsessed with never letting go of any of the men that she had dated. However, the last reading I did for her was when she finally had become engaged.

I also did some good work with Valise as she struggled with local government opposition towards her establishing a daycare service for dogs. Working with dogs was her passion, and I was glad to support her on this.

With all of my long-term clients, I believe I have contributed at least to their partial success, happiness, and well-being, but sometimes I feel I can only go so far with them and that it is time for them to find someone else, another psychic perhaps, who can help them—or, better yet, for them to learn to walk into their futures alone by using their own intuition.

I hasten to add, however, that any job dealing with people has its challenges and frustrations. Ask a therapist, or a lawyer, or a doctor.

Chapter Nine

Partying

When someone invites a tea leaf reader to do readings at a party, you can usually bet that it will be a good one. For one thing, no matter what we say, we are almost always found to be entertaining. I tend to give people something to talk about out of the ordinary small talk that is often part of people gathering together.

But also, if it is a large party, you can count on the fact that there will be many other out-of-the-ordinary entertainers. Like when I was invited to participate in an Arabian Nights theme party.

"Well, you have an authentic Arab in me," I explained to one of the three party planners who called to ask me to work there. She had just finished suggesting to me that I should dress in an Arabian-style costume.

I did not disappoint. I wore a multi-coloured, multi-wide-striped dress that flared out from just below the waist. It had glitters on it, too.

When I arrived at the party, I left my car along the side of the road as I had been instructed to do. I plunked my suitcase filled with tea cups, tea pots, tea, and crystals into the back of a shuttle van that drove me up to the house. ("We think it is going to rain," the party planner had told me. "The shuttle will make sure that you don't get your feet muddy.")

When I got out of the van and approached the house, I took a double take at the camel that was sitting next to the door. For a moment, I thought it was real because it was life size and the head was waving side to side. Coming up closer, of course, I saw it was a fake.

On entering, I saw that someone was practicing yoga with a couple of men, one of whom came up, shook my hand, and, through his introduction, made me realize he was one of the couple who was throwing the party. I never saw him again and never did meet his partner, but they paid me well for the readings I did there from about 8:30 p.m. to 1:30 a.m. the next morning, with maybe a fifteen-minute break.

People were great, though, throughout the night, bringing me amazing finger foods—like spelt bread with a slice of organic egg topped with caviar—and water and niceness. Not even minding waiting in line, which often happens when you are getting freebie psychic readings, they all chatted with each other happily as they waited

My lair was also amazing. All around me was floating brightly coloured silk, with changing coloured lights flashing through the silk. I sat behind a table while, one by one, those wanting readings came and sat across from me.

I had set up my cups and pots of tea at the bar. In another room, behind the bar, was the Tarot reader in the library. Down the hall were a massage therapist and a Jin Shin Do practitioner.

Upstairs, after the yoga was done, were an ongoing mood movie and belly dancers, followed by a DJ. I heard there were sunken baths somewhere else in the house, but I never managed to get far from my lair.

Apparently, there were three booze runs. One friend said they must have spent $15,000 on the party. When I left, my Third Eye was buzzing. This always happens when I do so many readings like that in a row. I feel punchy, like after drinking cups and cups of coffee all day. The energy feels blocked in my forehead, and I massage it myself (or someone else does if I'm lucky) until I feel tired enough to go to sleep.

When we picked up our cheques at the local hotel on the Monday, we were also treated to dinner there. What a party!

****

Early on in my career as a psychic, I was asked to do readings for a group of nurses who were holidaying at a resort. I ended up in the same room where the whole group had been eating their dinner, followed by (for some of them) several drinks.

The woman who had invited me and some of the others were very respectful and attentive to what I had to say as I gave readings one by one. But one quite drunk member of the group obviously did not believe in the authenticity of divination. While I read, she had ongoing commentary about how what I was saying was ridiculous. It really was difficult for me to believe in myself as I was giving the readings with this undercurrent of words oozing out of the mouth of the drunken woman. Her commentary went something like this: "Nothing like what she is #**% saying will ever happen."

From this experience, I realized that, in many people's minds, the entertainment aspect of having a psychic give readings at an event often overrides the underlying intrinsic value of getting a reading. Since then, I always ask to be in a separate room when giving readings to a group. There is, as well, another benefit in doing it this way. Whoever I am giving the reading to has his or her privacy. Each individual can go out after the reading and decide what she or he wants to share with the group and what will be kept secret from the others.

Another group I worked with often was one made up of teachers who took a weekend break in each other's company every spring. They were so interesting because every one of them wanted the reading to focus on someone (usually a son or daughter) in the family. I was amazed at how they were such caregivers that, given the opportunity to do something for themselves (in this case, get intuitive readings), they chose to defer to someone they cared about deeply instead of taking the time for themselves. Mind you, if I could help them sort out things about their children, I suppose it was helping them, too.

The other observation I have about this is the fact that these teachers, who had helped so many young people, were often feeling so defeated as to what to do to facilitate progress with those most near and dear to them. It seems to me that this is often the way in life. For those of us who are in the care giving fields (and I consider myself to be in this field as a psychic at least part, if not all, of the time), we often seek out or hope there is someone who will be there for our family members in the way that we are there for others. I guess someone who is detached from the person with problems or challenges is able to help that person best.

One time, when I did readings for this group of teachers, I had my pendulum with me. They were sitting together on couches. I went around the circle and asked them each a question that could be answered with a yes or a no. The motion of the pendulum (a crystal) on the end of a swinging chain determines if the answer is negative or positive. For example, a motion going west to east might mean no, and moving south to north might mean yes.

The group really enjoyed something that they could do for themselves. One of them phoned me the next day to ask where they could buy pendulums. (The usual place is in a metaphysical or New Age shop.) I felt good that I had given them a way to start getting control over asking the Universe for guidance. I think I helped empower them.

****

I have been invited to do readings at more than one bridal shower/stagette, and as I said earlier, I am always proud if I hear I was chosen instead of the male stripper.

At one I did in a city near where I live, every woman there was engaged, almost on-the-threshold-of-the-church-about-to-be-married, pregnant, or nursing a newborn baby. What struck me is that many of these young women wanted to get somewhere in their careers. Getting married, to them, was not the end of following their passions.

"At my job, will I ever be working in the actual area that I am trained in?" I remember one asking. "I mean, I just have so much to offer ..."

In all the readings, it seemed I addressed something with every one of them that focused on them keeping their sense of self.

I normally do not do large weddings, but one that I did is worth mentioning. "I usually find weddings quite boring," the organizer told me, which is why he decided to have a sort of carnival or circus atmosphere for the event.

He had someone doing card tricks; stilt-walking clowns; flame throwers; someone on the radio asking drivers, on boats passing by, to honk; a ferry boat honking; a biplane flying low above the outside event; and me in a tent, with a table inside for my tea cups, giving tea leaf and Tarot readings to several people who had never had a psychic reading before.

The ceremony itself featured a First Nations smudging ceremony; a marriage commissionaire, who tied the knot legally for the couple; and Tibetan Buddhists, who brought blessings and a song for everyone to sing. The Buddhists asked everyone present to send positive energy to the couple and requested them in turn to give those of us witnessing their marriage the same.

****

A couple of people connected to the First Nations communities near me attended my tea leaf reading workshops, and word got out among the communities about me. As a result, I was pleased to be invited to several of their special events.

One was a birthday party for a woman I will call Josie. It was to be a Mexican theme party as Josie and her husband often holidayed in that country. She also specifically wanted tea leaf reading (not Tarot) so she could get a chance to use her tea cups. Quite a few people have told me this—they want an excuse to pull out the cups that usually remain quite out of the way in a china cabinet. Often, these are cups that have been inherited and are beautiful, delicate heirlooms and worth a bit of money.

It was pouring rain at the party, but they had lots of tents up and I was reading in the house, as was the musician playing in the house with a sound system outside.

One man I remember well. I saw him struggling with a rock, and I saw if he would just let go of the struggle, he would be fine. At the end of the reading, he said, "That really resonated with me when you talked about the rock. I just stopped drinking two weeks ago." The message was "let go and let God." Try to be calm instead of struggling so hard, but also you then will become more detached, and the struggle will be less the longer you refrain from drinking.

When everyone gathered to feast, a man announced that those fifty or older should line up first at the buffet. I think this was the first time I had experienced elders recognized first instead of being left in the shadows of a large event, while the younger and more able beat them to the food.

It was considered a very important birthday for Josie because it was her fiftieth.

Besides this party, I have done readings at Indian and Metis Friendship Centre Christmas celebrations and Mental Wealth days. I like the term "mental wealth" because it suggests that being balanced mentally is wealth just as (or even more so than) having a lot of money is. These days are for staff who are counselors, social workers, and other caregivers for their community. I respect the way they recognize that they need nurturing in order to continue nurturing others.

At these events, there will be massage therapists, manicurists, and other healers as well. Things often come out in the readings about how discriminatory our society is. Like one woman telling me she really needed a new house and could not afford to get one herself, but that if she agreed to have the federal government's Indian Affairs department give her one, she would have to sign away her ancestral rights to the land. She was between a rock and a hard place.

Of course, in other ways, people are people. One woman who got a reading told me that that some First Nations people practice black magic. This is what her aunt, who lived next door to her, was doing to her, she said. Every culture has much good but can also have evil.

I do notice, when working with First Nations people, that the fact that spirit is involved in psychic readings is something that is so obvious to them that they never even need to discuss it.

Chapter Ten

Opening Third Eyes

I got into facilitating tea leaf reading workshops really soon after I started doing tea leaf reading. I did so because I had a decade of experience teaching writing courses focusing on most writing genres, with seniors as well as the general population. As I mentioned earlier, from this I concluded that, if you can teach well in one area, you can probably teach well in all areas, especially if you are passionate about what you are teaching.

Almost no one else facilitates tea leaf reading workshops, so I was freefalling when it came to designing one. The thing that stumped me the most was how to teach a person to understand the Reiki (energy healing) work I do before a reading starts, as well as what his or her intuition is and how it works.

It finally dawned on me that I needed to look very closely at what happens to me when I do a reading. The first thing that I do is what we practitioners of Reiki call second degree Reiki. It is sending energy to something that we want to happen. In this case, it is setting the energetic intention for an excellent, accurate, intuitive reading to happen.

The difficulty with this is that, to become a Reiki practitioner, a person has to be attuned by a Reiki master. I am a Reiki master, but to give people attunements at a tea leaf reading workshop that lasts a few hours is impossible.

So instead, I talk to my students about meditating (if they do already) or setting the intent for doing excellent, positive, intuitive readings with Reiki if they happen to be practitioners. The other option for all of them, I tell them, is to set the intent with positive affirmations.

On the day a reading is to be done, the tea leaf reader can say something like,

"Today, I do an excellent, accurate, intuitive tea leaf reading." The affirmation should be said three times, which is an important spiritual number. In Christianity, it is the three beings that make up God: the father, the son, and the holy spirit. But as I mentioned earlier, it goes way back in history as an important number for pagans; it is about bringing together the three energies of heaven, earth, and the ether energy between the two.

Also, the affirmation has to be said in the present tense. It has to be, "I do an excellent, accurate, intuitive tea leaf reading," and not, "I will do an excellent, accurate, intuitive tea leaf reading." If you say the affirmation in the future tense, you will always be working towards doing an excellent, accurate, intuitive tea leaf reading and never actually do it.

I coach them by explaining that the intuition is that flash (literally, I can see the yellow or white light that goes with it) of insight or inspiration. It comes into one's mind at the very second that the reader realizes what the image in the cup is. If you sit there and think and ponder over it, then you have already switched to the intellectual part of the brain. You are rationally trying to interpret what you are seeing. By doing this, you lose the intuitive flash and cannot get it back. You have to take the risk of saying what has flashed into your mind when it happens, before your reasoning makes you lose your courage.

The reason why courage is involved is that sometimes what you see and intuit seems so out there. But time and time again, the person who has drunk the tea will confirm that the "hunch" is totally correct based on the way his or her life is heading.

I always bring my special, deep-violet tablecloth with the mirrors on it that I bought at a Tibetan Buddhist evening of performance. I use it for the centerpiece of the table around which the participants sit in a circle. In the middle are my crystals—the clear quartz, to which I have given the intention to help me give accurate tea leaf readings; the rose quartz, for love; the ultraviolet crystal, to support the clarity of my Third Eye; a crystal quartz shaped like a heart; and a piece of Sedona, Arizona, red rock to help positive changes in our life to accelerate. More recently, a copper and a pink quartz pendulum have joined my other divination tools at the table.

I also arrange some of my multi-coloured tea cups around the crystals. My Tarot decks—the Rider-Waite and Osho Zen—are there, too. I put them on top of their carrying pouch with a silver elephant on it, one of my favourite exotic animals. I do this to transform the room—which is often a bland and even stuffy classroom or dull community recreational space—into a space for us to enjoy tea leaf reading and the magical energy that goes with it. The space becomes our space as diviners.

While we pass the cups around and read, our lives are revealed to each other. Suddenly, we see people as they are instead of what they look like. Sometimes, the ones that look the most conservative are the ones with the most "out there" stories.

I saw in the cup of one woman—who was dressed in a prim and proper business suit—that she bet on the horses. The reason I knew this was because I saw the horse that she should bet on had big, curled-up lips. It was probably named something like Little Miss Big Lips (you know, the strange names they call horses at the race tracks).

When we circulated one woman's cup, something about the Far East, with a man who came across as a shady character, kept coming up. The woman was warm and friendly. I did not intuit that she was of a criminal nature. After the reading was complete, she shared with the rest of us that her brother had been involved in criminal activity. She suspected he had purposely lost himself somewhere in Southeast Asia. At an advanced tea leaf reading workshop later in the year, she told us that her son had run into her nephew, who was the corrupt brother's son, and he confirmed everything that we had intuited.

Teaching tea leaf reading workshops has taken me to many interesting places. To tell you about them, I will make an exception to my rule to keep places confidential.

One really special place at which I have done workshops regularly and readings on many occasions is Milner Gardens in Qualicum Beach. The grounds and all the buildings on it were bequeathed to the Vancouver Island University (formerly named Malaspina University College), which has its main campus at Nanaimo but has teaching facilities in several mid-Vancouver Island communities, and even one in Powell River on the Sunshine Coast. It is an absolutely beautiful estate filled with all kinds of amazing plants, trees, and flowers, with many paths to walk through the forest. There is a two-story house, where the staff office is; a tea room; a kitchen; and classrooms. On the property is a gift shop, as well as cottages, gardens, and the home of the director, who lives on site with his family.

Prince Charles and Princess Diana visited Milner Gardens, as did Queen Elizabeth II and Prince Philip. I was told that the Queen and Prince Philip slept in different bedrooms while there. The feeling was that, when people live in palaces with fifty rooms, they can afford to sleep wherever they want to.

Apparently, it was Diana who discovered Milner Gardens. She was told about it by a wealthy Canadian woman friend who, I think, owns a chain of grocery stores. I guess the Royal Family is like any family when it comes to word-of-mouth. If one likes the place, she or he encourages other family members to visit.

When I do workshops at Milner Gardens, we have a delicious afternoon tea- style lunch, with egg salad sandwiches and squares of chocolate cake for dessert. Often, the lunch is served to us at a 300-year-old table. It is made of long, dark-brown wood and is surrounded by regal wooden chairs, with a big bouquet of freshly cut flowers as the centerpiece, as well as smaller bouquets in tea cups. One's feet can rest on a wooden railing at the base of the table. I am sure it still will be in existence, as strong and sturdy as ever, 300 years from now.

How I got to do workshops for Vancouver Island University (VIU) began when I phoned someone in the Continuing Education department. I asked her if she would consider the possibility of me doing a tea leaf reading workshop there.

"We don't do that kind of thing," she said, so quickly it sounded to me like she had not taken the time even to think about it. Really, this kind of thing is a form of discrimination against psychics.

"Well, you should," I shot back, just as quickly. "It will be very popular, and you will make a lot of money." She decided to take a risk, and soon I was regularly doing workshops at all five of the university's campuses.

This then helped me get into places like Selkirk College in the BC interior's Kootenay Mountains. Whenever I talk with a programmer, I get in the fact that I teach at VIU early on in the conversation, and this opens things up for me.

One other beautiful campus location where I do regular workshops is Royal Roads University, which is in Sooke, a community or suburb of Victoria, BC.

The buildings are elegantly historic, and the classrooms inside exude the same vibrations. Driving over winding roads and past majestic Douglas Fir trees is a communing-with-nature experience not soon forgotten. There are also flowers, shrubs, birds (including peacocks), and animals to match the beauty of each season. Interestingly enough, the people who take my workshops there have often been instrumental in me doing tea leaf reading gatherings elsewhere in Victoria.

But regardless of surrounding settings, enclosing any space that I work in with Reiki energy ensures that we will be in an excellent place to help our Third Eyes stretch open a little wider.

Chapter Eleven

Reading in Backrooms

The backrooms that I hang out in are the backrooms of metaphysical shops and tea rooms. They are usually storage rooms, really. Like most readers, I sit at a table there among the shop's stock. It helps ensure that the ego stays under control.

When I sit in these shops doing readings, it seems that I am contributing to or even extending the magic that the shops already provide. In return, my spiritual growth has really been nurtured in the New Age or metaphysical shops in which I do or have done readings. This is where I discovered Deepak Chopra, Louise Hays, Carolyn Myss, and so many other inspirational writers. Crystals and the power of pendulums have opened up to me while I have been putting in time in between readings at a variety of these shops. I have discovered an amazing array of Tarot cards in these shops; and heart cards, from which one can be picked each day to provide a message to boost the self-esteem; as well as angel cards that each display a one-word message that will manifest in your life each day.

Using expressions like "manifest" might not even be in my vocabulary if it were not for my relationship with metaphysical shops. I have met and done trades with many other psychics in metaphysical shops. Picked up gypsy-like jewelry in these places. Learned about and participated in sweet grass and sage smudging and other energy-cleansing techniques, as well as playing singing bowls to elevate healing vibrations.

Swapping stories of how spirit guides, fairies, and angels have influenced lives is something that has uplifted me often in New Age stores. Many come to these places to re-energize their spirits when their daily work life, or relationships, or whatever are dragging them down. Often, getting a reading or buying something from one of these shops gives the purchasers a feeling of joy that had been eluding them before entering the shop.

Really, each one of these shops is an oasis in the town or city where they are located. It is alright to talk in these places about fairies, angels, and communing with those who were once in body on the earth plane. Sometimes, a metaphysical shop is the only place people can "come out" as psychics, for example. I have been in shops where the owners do what they can to find newcomers rental housing and help them find work and become secure in a community.

In these shops, I have encouraged people to do homework following my readings. Once, I remember seeing a bear in someone's cup. He responded with, "Well, I am from California, and the bear is the state animal."

Intuiting it was more than this, I asked him to look in a book (for sale in the shop) on native spiritual interpretations of animal symbols. It turns out the bear represents creativity. This man was a highly creative filmmaker. (By the way, whether in a shop or at my home, I quite often encourage homework follow-ups, such as affirmations, or purchasing crystals, or getting bodywork done, to help people get what they need in life. I also help people strategize to get positive change. This is often like going through a rehearsal of what they can do in real life to bring this about.)

****

I remember once contacting a local Chamber of Commerce Visitor's Information to see if there was a metaphysical shop in one area where I was going to be doing a workshop. As is often the case, the volunteer working there was not at all sure if there was one of these in their town. I could hear him consulting with his co-worker before coming back to the phone. "Yeah, we have one," he said, with a smirk in his voice as he gave me the name, which alluded to wood spirits. He could not stop laughing; he thought the shop's name was that amusing.

Meanwhile, I was thinking, "That sounds like exactly the right place for me."

When I phoned them and asked about reading there, immediately they said yes. It was like they were just waiting for me to call.

In a way, they were because both of the owners are guided by spirit to do something good for their community. They are dedicated to putting joy into the lives of their family, friends, and neighbours. Through them, I see clearly that this is the same motivation for anyone who runs a metaphysical shop. Make your daily bread by doing something good for people. This is my motivation, too, so that is why doing readings in a shop like this is a perfect fit for me.

The second time I did readings there, I realized that I had gone to a new level in what I was doing and what Spirit was willing to give me in return. I did a six-day stint there, and by the second or third day, I started to see something was happening.

Almost everyone who came in was helping me with my spiritual awareness at the same time that I was helping them with theirs. They did not know that this was what they were doing, but they were.

Someone came in who was Capricorn, which is my astrological sun sign. Many of my insights about her life were connected to her dedication to caringly assisting everyone in her family—how she miraculously could fix and smooth the lives of those around her. But there was sometimes resentment from them—why can't she ever stumble like the rest of us? Why does she always have to be the best?

I got it. This is why people sometimes get so annoyed with me and unsupportive. It is: "She thinks she's so good, and she is so good, but I am sick of it."

When I completed my six-day visit to this metaphysical shop, one of the owners told me that she, too, had gone to a new spiritual level. I could see it on her face and, particularly, around her Third Eye. She was illuminated.

****

Being a tea leaf reader, the other places in which I have done my readings are tea rooms, such as the British-style silver service one that I began in and mentioned earlier. Besides this, I also can find a niche in shops that sell loose leaf tea. This is a revived phenomena as tea drinking, in recent years, has become more popular again after it declined for a while to latte coffee drinking.

These shops often have over one hundred tea varieties. The fringe benefit of doing readings in these places is having the opportunity to sample amazing black, green, and herbal teas. Each person who comes into the shop for a reading gets his or her choice of tea to drink. I always drink a cup of tea with each person for whom I do a reading. In a day, this can amount to trying half a dozen kinds of tea, and sometimes a lot more.

Being the Capricorn that I am, I often enjoy helping whoever is working in the shop, whether it is a tea or metaphysical shop. There are often times, and sometimes long time periods, when no one comes in and gets a reading. (Any psychic who tells you differently is not admitting to the reality of the work.) If times or the time of year is a financial down for people; if it is not tourism season or tourism is down; or even, sometimes, depending on the day of week, this can mean sitting for hours, as it can if there are lots of other psychics around competing with each other, or if a psychic comes into town from another area, or if the town is quite small and/or quite conservative.

I enjoy reading, so I often have a book on the go to help stave off the boredom, but after a while, even that can get boring. So occasionally, I will talk to customers about how wonderful certain New Age products are or rave about my favourite tea, depending what kind of shop I am in. I never lie. I do like a lot of what these shops have to offer.

Over the years, I really have become close to so many shop managers and staff as we often have lots of time to talk when the place is empty. We tend to open up to each other in a way that makes times that could be dull into fulfilling experiences. I enjoy the interaction with these shopkeepers because, since I am self-employed, I have no coworkers with whom to chat on a daily basis. Quite a few times, I have given them short readings to help them clarify something going on in their lives.

Chapter Twelve

Taking my Tea Cups on the Road

Whehen my son, Luke, got to the leaving-home-soon age, I started to fantasize about living the true gypsy lifestyle and travelling with my bag of tea cups, saucers, tea pots, Tarot cards, and crystals to wherever people beckoned me to do readings and workshops.

What I like about fantasies is they can become bigger as parts of them or smaller fantasies become realities.

So, first it was to get one or two workshops on Vancouver Island. Off and on, while I raised Luke, I had offered my tea leaf workshops on Salt Spring Island and, occasionally, in Victoria.

But Vancouver Island is a big island (or so I thought because I had stayed quite close to home while I was actively parenting). "Lots of possibilities to do workshops," I told myself.

I knew offering the workshops myself would mean renting a space wherever I wanted to go, getting posters up, and paying for advertising. Yet, if you never have been to a particular town before, it can be difficult even to find someone to put up the posters and to know when the best day to offer the workshop might be.

So, I chose to go quite a non-gypsy route with my travelling gypsy fantasy. Since I had taught for years in continuing education at a university and in a high school, as well as in recreation centres, when I facilitated the writing workshops, I thought I would try the same thing with my tea leaf reading workshops.

Once that programmer on Vancouver Island agreed to give me a try (after I persuaded her that it would be popular and make the university a lot of money), I decided to approach other branches of the same university. As I have said, it worked because I already had my foot in the door of the institution.

Around the same time, I tried a recreational centre up island in Courtenay. I had a friend living up there, so I knew I had a place to stay. Besides this, I have been a member of the Hostelling International Association since the 1970s, so I always have the option of a cheap bed to sleep in overnight.

When an institution decides to offer my workshop, I always nurture the process by sending out press releases to the local town newspapers. Often, small newspapers, especially, are looking for stories to fill up space, so the editor will print a short article based on my press release, with a photograph of me, at the very least. Many times, though, a reporter has interviewed me for an article that is run before the workshop or will attend my workshop and report on it.

Sometimes, programmers are quite amazed (and usually grateful, because it does not bode well for their institution if workshops are cancelled due to a shortage in enrollment numbers) when the workshop suddenly fills up because of an article that runs locally on the same week the workshop is scheduled.

One programmer told me once that publicity does not work this way—that it has to go out well in advance in order to get people to sign up. I have proven her wrong time and time again. In a one-day workshop like mine, it seems people do sign up at the last minute if they know or are reminded about it by an article run close to the workshop date. Maybe they do not register for it early because they are concerned that something "more important" might be happening on that weekend.

This is where my experience as a journalist has helped me develop my workshop facilitation in several locations. I sometimes get frustrated because lots of workshop instructors do not seem to realize that they need to promote what they are offering. It does not matter how interesting the workshop is or how good the facilitator is.

The other thing that works effectively (and does not cost me anything, just like the press releases do not) is putting a classified notice on Craigslist on the Internet.

When I go on these workshops and readings trips, I always try to do something enjoyable and see somewhere I have not seen before. This is why I love road trips.

Vancouver Island is so laden with forests; ocean, lake, and river water sparkling in the sunshine or swelling, as calm as a pregnant woman asleep, in the silence of sunset, with loons and ducks floating serenely on her belly.

When I was raising my son, I would watch the evening weather on television and wonder what all the places pointed out by the weather person were like. It was through my workshops that I was able to travel up to Courtenay and Comox; and then on to Campbell River; and north to where the road narrows and the scenery becomes more remote; ending in Port Hardy and swinging over to Port Alice before coming back down to my home on Salt Spring Island.

Now, when I hear about these places in the news, I know what they are like.

This is why travelling is good. It opens up the world for us. It is through my tea leaf reading that I have been able to venture out.

****

But, of course, once I get out there and see things so far, I always am called further. Like a true gypsy, I want more.

Where I was called next was to Nelson, BC. Right from the time I moved to the West Coast, I became curious about this city in the

Kootenay Mountains because so many people living on Salt Spring Island either moved from Nelson to our island or vice versa.

Now, I had found a way to go there for a visit and to have at least part of my trip paid for by doing readings and a workshop, as well as being able to declare expenses on my income tax. (I remember talking with an Australian in England who was amazed to hear that I had disclosed to the tax people that I am a tea leaf reader. Personally, I think we will never be accepted as a beneficial part of society unless we are open, even to government officials, as to who we are.)

I found a metaphysical shop in Nelson, which I thought I would because it is like Salt Spring Island, a psychic-friendly community. It also was run by a psychic named Thea Trussler, who specialized in Tarot. At first, when I e-mailed her, she did not respond, so I called her. On the phone, she said that she did not agree to hosting every intuitive who wanted to read there because, Thea explained, "You would not believe some of the people who turn up here."

I said I would be glad to give her a reading as a way for her to measure how accurate I am.

"Oh, no, that's fine," she said. "I can tell just by talking with you that you will do fine here." She was referring to what her intuition was telling her about me. I really got that what she said rang true.

Some of the very interesting work that Thea did in Nelson was connected to the historical Hume Hotel there. (Historical two-story homes and other buildings lined up in rows up the side of the city's mountain is one thing that makes Nelson so visually special.) She and other psychics spent many hours in the hotel in order to research the spirits who are overtly present in the building, according to the testimony of many of the staff there.

The result was a film of their findings called *Haunt at the Hume*. Thea, herself, did some Tarot readings in one of the hotel rooms. The staff said that people who stayed in that room, and others, regularly complained about encountering ghostly beings at night.

In the room Thea was in, she discovered through pulling cards that more than one couple, over the years, had met there to have love affairs. She found that, after the first couple spent time there, those who were tempted to have affairs were drawn to that room due to the energy it was exuding.

Thea gave me a reading in which she said she saw me meeting a very elderly tea leaf reader in France who would sort of pass the torch onto me as far as upholding our psychic gift. Later, I realized that Thea might have been seeing someone in Lebanon or, at least, of Lebanese background "crowning"' me to carry on. I think this because, in Lebanon, besides Arabic, people often speak French due to the fact that the country was once a colony of France.

Doing trades with psychics in Nelson has always been a highlight of my numerous trips there. Making a lot of money from tea leaf reading there has never been the case for me. I think this is because there are so many psychics in Nelson that there is a glut in the readings market. (The same thing sometimes happens on Salt Spring Island.) The perception that psychics have people waiting in line-ups to get readings from them, in general, is a bit of a falsity. To my knowledge, this sometimes happens when a psychic is doing readings free of charge or for a very low fee. I would rather charge the fee that I am worth and do an excellent job for fewer clients. Having said all this, although people do not line up around the block for a reading from me, I often have days jam-packed with readings.

This always has happened when I do readings at Dragonflies & Fairy Dust in Castlegar, which is a town half an hour away from Nelson. I believe this is because there are really no readers living in Castlegar, so the people there tend to come out for a visiting psychic as they can be few and far between there. Also, Dragonflies & Fairy Dust is the only metaphysical shop. In addition to this, the owners of the shop are very good at doing their jobs when it comes to making bookings. They get a percentage, so they realize that it is in their best interest to sign up people for readings. They also realize that people coming in for readings also will buy items from their shop when in there.

Spending time in Castlegar and the general area has helped me learn about the Doukabours, who came to Canada from Russia as they were pacifists who believed in farming cooperatively or communally. One of their descendants told me her grandmother used to do tea leaf reading. This may have been quite common, and this also could explain why what I do appeals to them.

Experiencing the East Kootenay Mountains is experiencing another kind of BC energy. In Nelson, people's groundedness is different than the more "floating around" or even "flying around" style of the West Coast. In Fernie, BC, near the Alberta border, the groundedness seems more immediately right-there-in-front-of-you, like the dynamic mountains that form a ring around the town.

I was there in May, the off-season between the downhill skiing in the winter and the mountain biking in the summer, but I did get the impression that whatever people tend to be doing, they are able to focus on it as if nothing else is happening around them. They are not easily distracted. You do what you are doing with intensity.

Those who have attended my workshops in Fernie and in nearby Kimberley have been very welcoming. Travelling psychics are few and far between there as these towns are off the beaten path and close to the more conservative province of Alberta, with perhaps more Christians who are of the psychics-are-doing-the-devil's-work variety.

I love going to places such as these. I probably feel a little like a cross between the show business people who used to travel with Chautauqua through the back road Canadian towns and villages during the Depression and the circus performers. As well, I feel a bit of something that is like the missionary's religious fervor. I like to connect with my kind of people, especially if they do not often get an opportunity to spend time with others who believe in the spiritual realm.

****

I have run across psychics who camp out in the bush or couch surf as they travel through parts of the world doing readings. It is probably the Capricorn in me that has made it impossible for me (to date anyway) to so casually enter communities to do readings in this way. I need to be grounded in the place. I need to know for sure that I will have clarity when giving someone a reading.

For this reason, as I have already said, I usually establish a place to do a workshop before going to a town. I also track down a shop where I can do readings. Doing publicity before arriving is also important to me. This is, after all, how I make my living.

When I went to Boulder, Colorado, it was a bit of a different situation. I still grounded myself there, but doing psychic work in that gorgeous Rocky Mountain city evolved out of a house/dog/cat-sitting gig.

Before embarking on it, I was not at all sure if I would do a workshop or even any readings when I got there. I had very little money at the time so took the Greyhound bus there.

Let me say that most people nowadays would not consider doing anything else but taking an airplane over a state like Wyoming, for example. I am here to tell you that anyone who does this is missing out on a breathtakingly beautiful landscape. Rolling hills with platinum blonde grass spans out in every direction, as far as the proverbial eye can see. Here and there are surprises: bison grazing in a coulee between two hills, or a piece of installation art, or a stunning sunset. In a bus, I found I could gaze at the surrounding natural beauty to my heart's content. The bus driver was the one that had to keep his or her eyes on the road.

When I got to Boulder, I found it to be my kind of place. For a start, it is a university town, which, in the United States, often is synonymous with being a mecca for progressive people.

Many of the successful business people were old hippies and proud of it. I remember hearing an advertisement on the radio from a housing developer who was proud to identify himself as such.

Of great interest to me was the Celestial Seasonings tea company, located on Sleepy Time Lane (named after the company's most popular tea—chamomile). Inside, photographs with text under them tell the story of how the founder began gathering his first tea from herbs growing around Boulder and Colorado Springs. He would sell it in muslin bags at the Saturday markets.

The photograph of the company's first art department staff tells a story that words might not be able to get across. "My God, they were all a bunch of hippies," I said to myself as I stared at the young grinning faces and bodies in groovy clothing.

I found a metaphysical bookstore there that was glad to have me do readings at their psychic fair on Saturdays. Among the book aisles, a variety of us intuitives set up with our cups, crystals, and other trade paraphernalia. Again, this was the ideal situation for us to do trades in between paying customers.

Through someone connected to my dog-sitting gig (by the way, one of the rangiest dogs I ever took care of—I took him on four walks a day in order to try to deal with how hyper he was), I found a wonderful spiritual centre where I was able to do a tea leaf reading workshop. Among those I met there were people connected to the Buddhist retreat centre, a Chi Gong expert and author, and someone who had travelled on the El Camino pilgrimage in northern Spain.

****

From as early as the second year that I was doing tea leaf readings, other intuitives have predicted that I would go around the world doing my work. When the first person—a woman who was taking a workshop from me—predicted this global mission, I do not think I realized that what she was referring to were my readings.

Finally, in my tenth or eleventh year, there were at least three psychics who renewed this theme of me taking my tea cup reading skills around the world.

How I was going to do this, I did not know. I do make a living primarily as a tea leaf reader, but many would say it is a miracle that I am able to scrape together any kind of income doing this. (Most readers dabble in it and hold down other jobs.) To be able to fly around the world, to me, was beyond belief.

Still, sometimes, intuitive predictions need to be said yes to by the person who has received the reading. Maybe some predictions are so big that we not only have to have faith in them but have to take steps to give them the green light.

So, when I planned my trip to England and Scotland in 2008, I decided to try to break into Europe as a reader. At first, I did not know what to do as I had no understanding of how being a psychic would work on that continent. I had been there before but not as a tea leaf reader.

Then, I realized that it would work for me if I grounded myself in the process. I would go about doing it the same way that I lined up readings and workshops closer to home.

I went to the Internet and searched for metaphysical shops in the cities I knew I was going to be visiting. In Glasgow, I found one, and when I looked at its website, it seemed very familiar to me. There were the crystals, books, Tarot cards, etc., similar to the contents in any of the many New Age shops in which I have been and done readings.

I made a point of getting out of bed early enough to be coherent on the telephone at seven in the morning, which is late afternoon in the United Kingdom. The shop owner was such a friendly woman and agreed right away to me doing a workshop and readings there. One of her regular psychics was kind enough to back out of her regular Sunday spot so I could be there.

I had to walk a long way from the hostel where I was staying (and got lost once) before I found my way to the place, but other than that, it was just like doing readings and workshops at home. As usual, I sent positive Reiki energy ahead of time so everything would go well. I did not let myself think that they would find I had a funny accent; or that I was in a country that, up until a few days before, I had never been in and in a huge city that I had never visited until I got there the day before. I did not think about the possibility that I might not be of the "right" class. I just did what I love doing so much, and everything fell into place.

I felt I was giving back to those Scottish tea drinkers something that had long been in their ancestry before I came along. So, I proved to myself that I could do it overseas.

Before leaving on the trip, I also had tried to line up something in England. In London, a metaphysical shop owner was fine with me doing tea leaf reading there. Just one stipulation: I had to be willing to do it permanently for one or maybe two days a week. I do have an inkling that the Universe was nudging me to move to London, but I was not prepared to heed its call—not yet, anyway.

****

I even have gone to Canada's North with my tea cups and pots in tow. A friend was going to a conference in Whitehorse, Yukon, and asked me if I wanted to come along. Turned out, due to commitments, I could not go to the conference, but the wheels had been set in motion, so I went ahead and booked a flight for a week in the land where the Klondike Gold Rush took place in the 1800s.

The programmer at the recreation centre who agreed to schedule my workshop was a bit skeptical. She said that, because it is dark for such a large chunk of the year, people do not want to be tied down to doing workshops in the summer time. They are off holidaying, out on the land and water.

Having spent way too many winters in Winnipeg's minus-forty weather, I doubted very much as to whether I would want to venture into the snow and ice zone and darkness of the Yukon. The summer midnight sun was much more appealing to me.

The programmer helped me, though, by putting up posters around the city. And, as often happens, people waited until the last week or two to register, but then they did to the tune of more than my fifteen-person workshop limit. To add to this, the programmer had persuaded me that a three-hour workshop would go over better in the summer. So, I had more than my maximum and was short two of the total five hours that my workshop usually runs.

I cut back on my introductory chitchat about how I became a tea leaf reader, and we focused on what the workshop was really about: making sure everyone did at least some reading of the leaves and got at least a short reading each. This workshop, along with two days of readings at an herbal shop, paid for my airplane fare and accommodation.

For the other four days of my visit, I connected with Mother Earth. I walked the Millennium Trail, which is a three-kilometer path along two sides of the mighty Yukon River. It was built in 2000, realizing the dream of a Roman Catholic priest, who arrived in the Yukon in the 1940s and believed there should be a place for everyone, regardless of their abilities, to get out into nature.

I took a tour to the Yukon Wildlife Preserve and sketched the animals—bison, elk, caribou, mountain goats, musk ox, moose, mountain sheep. The day before, I had viewed most of these species stuffed and mounted in the McBride Museum, where the cabin of Sam McGee is also on view. Contrary to popular belief, the subject of Robert Service's famous poem was from Canada and not from Tennessee, U.S.A. Of course, the poem was highly fictionalized.

As well, I did the tour of the SS Klondike, the first paddlewheel boat to ply the river between Whitehorse and Dawson. I even went to a hot springs on the invitation of a woman I ran into who had attended my workshop.

It seems Opal, as I will call her, is meant to follow in my footsteps and brought out a bit of mentoring in me (which is starting to happen more and more). She told me she had always wanted to do tea leaf reading. So I gave her one of my tea cups—something I have never done before, as I am so attached to them.

After the workshop and the private reading I gave her, I bumped into her at a used-book store. "I was just thinking about you," she said, as she appeared out of the stacks, having heard my distinctive voice while I talked with the owner.

She had just found a mint condition copy of a tea leaf reading book that I always recommend to students. Mine has been in tatters for years, and I had not seen another copy of this book since I purchased mine. To top it off, the bookstore owner gifted it to her.

Just like when I started, synchronicity seems to be with Opal to realize her dream. In other ways, she is experiencing a similar life to mine. She had done lots of travelling and then became a single parent in her early thirties, as it was with me.

One of the reasons why I decided to do workshops—to ensure that tea leaf reading continues after I leave this earth plane to transcend into the spirit world—seems to be happening.

Chapter Thirteen

Day-to-Day Life and Practical Magic

One of the many things that I enjoy about what I do is that each day is grounded in my tea leaf reading work, but often I do not know the details of what each day I live is going to be like even when I am not on the road but back home. Each day is different and often brings the unexpected.

If I do have morning readings or other work-related matters that I need to deal with immediately, I usually meditate and do exercises after I wake up each morning. These, I find, are crucial to maintaining my clarity and accuracy as a tea leaf reader, as well as to maintaining my health.

On one day, I will do self-healing Reiki and energy cleansing for my chakras (the energy centres in the body that correspond to different aspects of our lives and are derived from the Hindu faith). I breathe happiness, love, and bliss into each of my chakras while meditating on the mantra: "I am happiness, love, and bliss."

I also recite the Reiki principles to myself: Just for today, do not worry. Just for today, do not anger. Honour your parents, teachers, and elders. Earn your living honestly. Show gratitude for every living thing.

Reminding myself of these principles over the years has stopped my obsessive worrying, lessened my anger, and helped me to reconcile with my parents and to be a wiser person, to do the best job I can in my readings, and to respect and love everything natural.

I then send energy to my son, Luke, directing it to areas of his life that he would like to develop and so that he can live with happiness, love, and bliss. It is my long-distance parenting.

Then, I direct Reiki energy to areas of my own life that I want to expand.

I do all of the above every other day.

On alternate days, I do spiritual readings after I wake up. These include affirmations, meditative readings, and chanting. Then, I do a number of exercises, which include Chi Gong, Tai Chi, and Yoga.

I think the reason why people sometimes do not practice these healing-by-energy disciplines is because they believe they have to do them for a long time each day and know all of the stances or poses in order to benefit. I benefit from doing them for only a few minutes.

I also do some toning exercises with light weights.

All of this might sound obsessive. I believe I need to do these things in order to continue to do my readings and do them with clarity. In doing psychic readings, I expend a huge amount of energy. I have to do these things to rejuvenate myself.

Then, I eat a late breakfast, shower, and go to my computer. Among my e-mails are often those from people who want to line up in person or for long-distance readings. Sometimes, they want to know when I will be coming back to their town.

There is a door knock. Someone, who I have probably never met before, is standing there. She or he wants to know if I have time to do a reading.

The phone rings with the same inquiry. Do I have time to do a reading today, next week, or even next month?

Of course, if I already have readings booked for the day, I do all of the above things around my readings.

I usually try to go for a walk just before supper in order to unwind and to ground myself to the earth, as a Capricorn loves to do. Occasionally, I will get a regular client dropping by in the evening to get a short reading; or a visitor to my community might knock or phone in the evening to see if I just might be available because they just happened to be passing by and noticed my sign, or they cannot book for any other time as they are departing the area early the next morning.

I would like to point out here that I trust the Universe to provide me with the readings I need to pay my bills each month. However—as you can imagine—bills have deadlines that do not always correspond with the days in the month when most of my money from readings comes in. I do not get a bi-weekly pay cheque.

It would be nice if those to whom I owe money would be more flexible to match my cash flow. My long-suffering landlord is, but most others are not.

It also would be nice if the institutions for which I do tea leaf and Tarot workshops would be more flexible with their schedules in order to pay me promptly. Some are, and I truly thank them.

It also would be nice if my credit union would recognize that self-employed people like me should be able to get a line of credit.

Why should I have to contend with debt in a negative way in order to have the freedom to work at my passion? Society needs to take a look at this, especially at a time in history when fulltime jobs are starting to become a thing of the past. Society has to more widely respect what psychics do.

Meanwhile, I continue to enjoy my days when I am at home, with the Universe helping me to mold each day in its own unique way. It is usually during the days that I am working out of my home that I connect with people who just want insight on something they need to do on a practical level. I can help because the Universe provides me with an array of information that will help my clients in whatever areas the Universe sees that they need help.

When Jackie phones me concerning where she should buy a house, she asks me about specific places. I respond, using my intuition and divination tools, by saying something like this: "The house you have looked at in Oak Bay will need to be cleansed, as the people who lived in it were always arguing ... One in North Vancouver is in a good community for you to make lots of friends, but you will have to establish strong boundaries in order to get your own work done ... In White Rock, I see the house you might buy would be a target of lots of crime ... On Pender Island, you will constantly be reminded of your ex-husband because lots of people know him there ... Gibson's would be okay, but you will spend a lot on renovations."

If Betsy phones about whether her son should marry the young woman who he impregnated, I might pull the death Tarot card, to which she will respond, "I take it that he should not marry her." I also might see in the tea leaves that she needs to distance herself from the young people's relationship and focus on being a grandmother.

Gisele might ask which health practitioner to go to for her leg. I might see a physiotherapist, but the next person who comes with this request I might tell to go to an acupuncturist. Each person is different, and her or his needs are different.

Philip might ask when his insurance settlement will take place. I might see that he has to fill out a form. "When you fill out a form," I say.

Joan might ask how much her settlement is going to be. "Fifty thousand dollars," might roll across the intuitive Rolodex in my mind's eye. I tell her I see that this will be the amount.

Sometimes, I just volunteer some practical information. When I was giving Jolene a reading at her funky little house, surrounded by her beautiful art with its misty dream-like quality, the voice in my head whispered, "She will sell a painting tomorrow."

I had just told her I would be visiting the art show in which her work was featured, along with many other artists. I hesitated for a moment, but I am nothing if not gutsy. "You will sell a piece of art tomorrow," I said.

I would face the music, I decided, if she did not sell one.

The next day, I spent over an hour visiting the outdoor art show. Lots of paintings, but I did not see money being exchanged for any of the art. To find Jolene, I had to ask, so I did not walk up to her spot until late afternoon.

There she was, standing next to a young woman who was holding one of her pictures, all wrapped up, as Jolene had just sold it to her. After the woman left with her acquisition, I nudged Jolene. "So you sold a painting," I said.

"Yes," she said. "Earlier, someone bought one, but that didn't count because she had talked about getting it for days. Then, I sold another one."

As I left, Jolene pointed me out to an artist friend of hers. "That's my psychic," she said. "She predicted I would sell a painting today."

The work I do is so enjoyable. It is magical in a zillion ways. Every time I sit down to do a reading, I never know what might happen. That is what makes it so exciting and, dare I say, unpredictable for me. I often am just as surprised by the information that is channelled through me as the person who is getting the reading.

Life is magical. Live in the light. Enjoy good energy.

Acknowledgements

I thank each person to whom I have given a tea leaf reading. I also thank everyone who has provided places for me to do readings or to offer my workshops. You warm my heart, and the spirit in me honours the spirit in you.

I thank my friends who have supported me so that this book could actually be published. They include my mother, Anne Lester; Chris Anderson; Candace Holmstrom; and Kim Hunter. Your assistance in helping me bring my two passions—tea leaf reading and writing—together in book form is honourable.

I thank Sandy Zaccagnino of Goldin Copyediting Services for her caring, sensitive book editing approach. I recognize spirit in you.

I thank Chad Lilly and InnerCircle Publishing for providing the vehicle through which I am able to get my book out there to readers around the world. Your vision rings true.

Tanya Lester
Salt Spring Island, BC, Canada
January 2010

Bibliography

A Highland Seer. *Tea-Cup Reading and the Art of Fortune-Telling by Tea-Leaves.* New York: George Sully and Company, 1968.

Chopra, Deepak, MD. *Creating Affluence: Wealth Consciousness in the Field of All Possibilities.* San Rafael, California: New World Library, 1993.

Conroy, Joseph F. and Emilie J. Conroy. *The World in Your Cup: A Handbook in the Ancient Art of Tea Leaf Reading.* Eagleville, Pennsylvania: DNA Press, LLC, 2006.

Hallowell, Gerald, ed. *The Oxford Companion to Canadian History.* Don Mills, Ontario: Oxford University Press Canada, 2004.

Hewitt, William W. *Tea Leaf Reading.* St. Paul, Minnesota: Llewellyn Publications, 1992.

Myss, Caroline, Ph.D. *Anatomy of the Spirit: The Seven Stages of Power and Healing.* New York: Three Rivers Press, 1996.

Aware Talk Radio

Join Us - LIVE - 7 Nights A Week!!!

Or Listen To Past Archives @:

www.innercirclepublishing.com

http://www.blogtalkradio.com/aware

Call In Number: *(646) 716-8138*

Aware Talk Radio incorporates all fields of science, from the normal to the paranormal, from the physical to the metaphysical. We seek to expand the awareness of humankind. Your Comments, Questions, and Guest Suggestions are welcome.Aware Talk RadioCall In Number: (646) 716-8138

LaVergne, TN USA
07 September 2010
196161LV00004B/123/P